Great Men of Essex

DESERT ISLAND LOCAL HISTORIES:

Great Men of Essex   1-874287-41-4
Essex in 1950   1-874287-42-2

DESERT ISLAND FOOTBALL HISTORIES:

Aberdeen: The European Era   1-874287-11-2
The Book of Football: A History to 1905   1-874287-13-9
Bristol City: The Modern Era   1-874287-28-7
Cambridge United: The League Era   1-874287-32-5
The Story of the Celtic 1888-1938   1-874287-15-5
Colchester United: From Graham to Whitton   1-874287-27-9
Coventry City: The Elite Era   1-874287-03-1
Coventry City: An Illustrated History   1-874287-36-8
England: The Quest for the World Cup   1-897850-40-9
History of the Everton Football Club 1878-1928   1-874287-14-7
Halifax Town: From Ball to Lillis   1-874287-26-0
Hereford United: The League Era   1-874287-18-X
Ireland: The Quest for the World Cup   1-897850-80-8
Luton Town: The Modern Era   1-874287-05-8
Luton Town: An Illustrated History   1-874287-37-6
Peterborough United: The Modern Era   1-874287-33-3
Portsmouth: From Tindall to Ball   1-874287-25-2
Portsmouth: Champions of England 1948-49 & 49-50   1-874287-38-4
The Story of the Rangers 1873-1923   1-874287-16-3
Red Dragons in Europe   1-874287-01-5
The Romance of the Wednesday   1-874287-17-1
Scotland: The Quest for the World Cup   1-897850-50-6
Stoke City: The Modern Era   1-874287-39-2
West Ham: From Greenwood to Redknapp   1-874287-19-8
West Ham: The Elite Era   1-874287-31-7
Wimbledon: From Southern League to Premiership   1-874287-09-0
Wimbledon: From Wembley to Selhurst   1-874287-20-1
Wimbledon: The Premiership Years   1-874287-40-6

DESERT ISLAND TRAVELS:

The Virgin Whore: Tiananmen, Travels & Traumas   1-874287-23-6
To Dream of Pigs: Travels in South & North Korea   1-874287-02-3

THE DESERT ISLAND DRACULA LIBRARY:

The Primrose Path   1-874287-21-X
Dracula: Sense & Nonsense   1-874287-24-4
Dracula: The Shade & the Shadow   1-874287-10-4
Dracula: The Novel & the Legend   1-874287-04-X
The Origins of Dracula   1-874287-07-4
Treatise on Vampires & Revenants   1-874287-06-6
Dracula Unearthed (annotated)   1-874287-12-0
The (annotated) Shoulder of Shasta   1-874287-30-9
The (annotated) Jewel of Seven Stars   1-874287-08-2
The (annotated) Lady of the Shroud   1-874287-22-8
Snowbound: (annotated) The Record of a Theatrical Touring Party   1-874287-29-5
A Glimpse of America   1-874287-35-X

GREAT MEN OF ESSEX

by

C HENRY WARREN

SERIES EDITOR: CLIVE LEATHERDALE

Desert Island Books Limited

First Published in 1956 by The Bodley Head

This edition published in 2000
by
DESERT ISLAND BOOKS LIMITED
89 Park Street, Westcliff-on-Sea, Essex SS0 7PD
United Kingdom
www.desertislandbooks.com

British Library Cataloguing-in-Publication Data
A catalogue record for this book is available from
the British Library

ISBN   1-874287-41-4

Printed in Great Britain
by
Redwood Books, Trowbridge, Wiltshire

Contents

		Page
	Series Editor's Note	6
1.	Thomas Paycocke	7
2.	William Harvey	20
3.	John Ray	35
4.	Dick Turpin	56
5.	John Constable	74
6.	William Morris	91
7.	Captain Oates	112

Series Editor's Note

It is a privilege to make available once more Clarence Henry Warren's portrait of seven great Essex lives. Part of the book's charm is that it was penned by a man born in the nineteenth century and shaped by its culture. Warren writes gentlemanly things about those under his gaze and was probably a gentleman himself. Of Captain Scott's doomed attempt to reach the South Pole in 1912 – which provided Warren with Captain Oates' famous act of valour to set before the reader – hc can find little to criticise. The author cannot even bring himself to censure Dick Turpin, prince of highwaymen. True enough, Warren records his mis-doings, but employs the language of regret rather than that of condemnation. One can almost sense Warren's discomfort at the title of his book: Turpin could hardly be called a 'great' man. 'Great' Men should perhaps read 'Famous (or Infamous)' Men in Turpin's case.

These essays could probably not have been written in our blunt modern age, with its politically correct disdain for biographies of 'dead, white males' and its altered priorities, which would demand insight into the sexual peccadilloes of those under discussion as a means of assessing and explaining their lives. Warren would probably be shocked at the way modern biographers go about their business.

The lives presented to us could hardly be more varied. Warren goes for the tinker, tailor, soldier, sailor method of selection. His book is valuable not only for resurrecting Essex lives, some of whom may be unfamiliar to modern readers, but also for the sheer pleasure of Warren's prose.

Clive Leatherdale
Desert Island Books

Thomas Paycocke

ANYONE VISITING the Eastern Counties for the first time will surely be surprised at the unusual size of some of the village churches. Thaxted, Lavenham, Long Melford, Dedham – the churches in these out-of-the-way villages are altogether disproportionate to the populations they serve. From a distance they almost seem to be standing alone in the fields; and when he comes nearer, the visitor finds only a few houses clustered round the giant edifice.

How did it come about that these enormous churches were built in such remote, tiny places?

And there is another surprising thing about them, besides their unusual size. They are unexpectedly ornate and beautiful – architecture with a flourish. The cost of erecting and decorating them must have been very great indeed; and from where, in these little villages, could such wealth have come?

The answers to these questions are bound up in the fact that once upon a time the villages were larger and far more prosperous. Fossil villages is the term sometimes (and perhaps a little unfairly) applied to them today; but in the fourteenth, fifteenth and sixteenth centuries they were very much alive.

That was the time when the Cloth Trade of this country was second to none in the world; and the three centres upon which it chiefly concentrated were East Anglia, Yorkshire and the West Country. Thaxted, Dedham, and the rest of the diminished Essex villages teemed with workers in those days, all of whom were in one way or another associated with the manufacture of woollen cloth. They were spinners, weavers, dyers, fullers, shearmen, and so on, each contributing his special process within the total job.

Out of this prosperity flowered these vast and lovely churches – a fact that is remembered today in the name by which they are commonly called: the 'Wool' churches. But even if there were more people to use them, they must still have been much larger than was necessary; and to explain this we have to search for another factor.

This further factor was the prodigious wealth of just a few men in whose capable hands the whole set-up of the cloth trade lay. The ordinary villager was no better off, relatively, than his counterpart today: it was his employers – one or two in every village, or even in every district – who reaped the benefits of this great prosperity. Indeed, their wealth grew, in some cases, to quite princely proportions. They were called the Clothiers; and it is to them, rather than to the greater size of the population in those days, that we owe the 'Wool' churches.

It should be remembered that England was then a Catholic country. That men of substance and power should bequeath a liberal share of their riches to the church was nothing unusual: it was, in fact, enjoined upon them to do so. Thereby they might salve their consciences and save their souls. Very likely the gift had in it an element of self-glorification: it would be surprising if this were not so; but the prime intention of the Clothiers in contributing so liberally towards the erection of these great churches was, no doubt of it, to glorify God.

Fortunately these wealthy merchants were also men of good taste. Their lavishness was used to fine purpose. If there was an element of display in the way they spent their money on these churches, at least it found expression in an architecture of exceptional beauty. Gazing today at the 'Wool' churches, with their soaring proportions, their carven stone chantries delicate as lace, their oaken roofs and jewelled windows, we can well afford to forgive those Clothiers their moment of pride.

But for the flourishing wool cloth trade, then, these great buildings would never have existed. 'Among all crafts,' said a writer of the time, 'this was the only chief, for that it was the greatest merchandize, by the which our country became famous throughout all nations.'

Not cloth, but the wool itself, grown on the backs of English sheep, had hitherto been the chief export. In the thirteenth and fourteenth centuries sheep, in fact, were the basis of English farming. The Manor had its flock; the great religious houses up and down the country had their flocks; even the poor peasant numbered a precious sheep or two among his few possessions.

The wool was sent over to Flanders and to Italy, to be woven into cloth on the looms of Bruges and Ypres, Ghent and Florence. From there it was sold all over Europe. It even came back to England, so that, as Eileen Power says, 'the Englishman of the Middle Ages wore a coat of English wool, but it had been woven in Flanders.'

Gradually, however, all this was changing. Already under William the Conqueror and his Flemish wife skilled weavers were being encouraged to come over here from Flanders to weave English wool on the spot; and yet more came over in the reign of Edward III, enjoying the special protection of the Crown; until, by the fifteenth century, the English manufacturers of cloth rivalled those of the Netherlands.

Not wool, but the cloth itself, became now the country's chief export and the firm foundation of its wealth.

Time and time again, throughout its history, England has, by choice as well as by force, opened its gates to let the foreigner in; and perhaps the process was never more beneficial to the country as a whole than now, when the master weavers of the Netherlands, with their accompanying apprentices and journeymen, enriched England with their skills.

Enriched England – and themselves too, of course. At least, some of them. For it was not the weavers themselves, the actual makers of the cloth, who benefited, so much as their masters, the astute merchants who bought up the stocks of wool, making a corner in it, as we say today, and then delivered it to the weavers to weave it into cloth, to the fullers to full it, and to the shearmen to finish it off, receiving it all back again as the finished article, ready for export.

These merchants, in fact, growing wealthy on other men's work, were the first capitalists – in a pre-capitalist age. They were the *nouveau riche* of their day. They saw their chance and had both the courage and ability to grasp it, reaping enormous rewards as a result.

The *entrepreneur,* (writes G M Trevelyan, in his *English Social History)* with a more than local outlook and with money at his command, was required to collect the raw material, the half-manufactured and the finished article, and pass them on from craftsman to craftsman and from place to place, from village to town, from town to port, and finally to bring a standardized article to the best market. For all this capital was needed.

As their capital grew, so these merchant adventurers began to employ more and more men and women in the villages, until presently almost the entire local community depended upon them for its livelihood. To quote Eileen Power, who made the study of the Middle Ages her life's work, 'their servants carried wool to the cottages for the women to card and spin; carried the spun yarn in turn to dyers, weavers, fullers, shearers; and carried the finished piece of cloth back to the industrial middleman – the cloth-ier, as he was called – who in his turn disposed of it to the mercantile middleman, who was called a draper.'

This system was known as the 'putting out' system, or out-work, and it persisted in the English countryside up to the time of the Industrial Revolution when the trade shifted from the country to the town, from the cottage to the factory; and the wool villages of East Anglia, Yorkshire and the West Country, once so busy and thriving, diminished almost at a throw to the small, silent villages as we know them today.

One or two of the great Clothiers of the fifteenth and sixteenth centuries stood out even above the general run of these wealthy and influential merchants. Such, for instance, was William Grevel of Chipping Campden in the Cots-wolds: such also was Thomas Spring of Lavenham in Suffolk. Both these men attained to such influence that theirs were household names all over the kingdom; and the villages where they lived, the stone village of Campden and the timber and plaster village of Lavenham, owed their one-time prosperity, as today they still owe their architectural charm, to the Clothiers who practically ran them.

But our concern here is with another Clothier, equally rich if not perhaps quite so widely known, Thomas Paycocke of Coggeshall in Essex.

It is impossible to realise, as one walks the quiet streets of Coggeshall today, that this was one of the most prosperous centres of the English cloth trade in the fifteenth and sixteenth centuries. All the industries it can boast now are a little brewing; the making of isinglass, gelatine and glue; and, in the neighbouring fields, much seed-growing.

Yet there are still many lovely old houses in the streets, belonging to a wealthier day; and, most of all, there is still Paycocke's own house, a glory of carved timber, close against the main road, to remind us of the time when his weavers' looms clacked in every cottage and the entire population looked to him as master and benefactor.

Paycocke's house is now in the charge of the National Trust that takes care of so many of our fine old buildings which would otherwise be spoiled or, worse, pulled down; and anybody who is curious to see it may do so. As he roams through the heavily timbered rooms, with their carved beams, their exquisite oak panelling and their great open hearths, the visitor will at least get some idea of how the great Clothiers lived.

'Such mansions in the village street,' as Trevelyan reminds us, '... mark the rise of a new rural class, as wealthy as the neighbouring gentry with whom they were not long in forming marriage alliances, and whose privileged circle they entered by the purchase of landed estates.'

History is to be found not only in the written word. Often, indeed, it was never recorded in books at all. Excavations, for example, are today uncovering much of our island's early story that we knew nothing about when the written word was our chief evidence.

And so it is with Thomas Paycocke and his family. His life story was never written down, and only the patient industry and loving curiosity of certain scholars have enabled us to know the man even as well as we know him now – and that is not very much. They found his story principally in three things: the village church where he worshipped and was buried; the house in which he lived; and the detailed Will wherein he remembered all his friends.

At first sight this would not seem much to work on; but it is the historian's task to read between the lines, to interpret the slightest hint, and to build up from such fragments (ignoring nothing as being too insignificant) a portrait of the man and of the time and place and circumstances in which he lived. This is what has been done in the case of Thomas Paycocke until he – and indeed all the Paycocke family – stand revealed to us across the centuries.

And further, we may see in him the type of the great Clothiers of his day.

Although Thomas Paycocke was the first of the family to live in the house that now bears their name, he was not the first to settle in Coggeshall and lay the foundations of its prosperity. It was, in fact, his father, John Paycocke, who built the house, probably giving it to his son on the occasion of his marriage to Margaret Harrold. At any rate, it is Margaret's and Thomas's initials that are carved here and there on the beams.

The Paycockes originally came from Clare, a village just over the border in Suffolk, not far away, where they were grazing butchers, men of more substance than such a calling would seem to imply, for they owned much property scattered about the countryside and were already quite rich. It was somewhere about the middle of the fifteenth century that a branch of the family moved over to Coggeshall and settled there.

From butcher grazier to clothier was, indeed, an expected transition, since the whole economy of England at this time was gradually shifting over from sheep-farming, for the production of wool as well as meat, to cloth-making.

Nor was the move to Coggeshall any more surprising, for almost certainly the Essex village was already engaged in the cloth trade, Colchester, one of its greatest and earliest centres, being only a few miles away. Moreover, for some time now the manufacture had in general been moving out from the towns into the country: so much so, in fact, that by 1622, when Fuller published his *Worthies of England* he was to describe the whole countryside as 'like Bethsheba, "she layeth her hand to the spindle and her hands to the distaffe" ... It will not go amiss to pray that the plough may go along, and the wheel around, that so (being fed by the one and clothed by the other) there may be, by God's blessing, no danger of starving in our nation.'

Like all men who suddenly achieve great wealth and position, John Paycocke, as one of the first of this new and vastly influential rural class, was very conscious of his position. The house he built for Thomas and Margaret is evidence of that. A more ornate building, for its modest size, both inside and out, can scarcely be imagined. It is impossible to pass through the little street where it stands, close against the road, without staring in amazement and delight.

But listen to Eileen Power's description of it. She knew the house as those of us who visit it can never do, for she once lived in it for a while. Here is what she says:

Whoever enters it knows at once that generations have lived in it ... The house is drenched with humanity, so that you can live alone in it for weeks and not feel lonely ... You need never feel shy of Paycocke's; it knows its business too well; and only a less perfect and less seasoned house would allow you to feel an intruder in the home of Thomas Paycocke ... These beauties are of the spirit; but it has no lack of the superficial beauties. Thomas Paycocke has somehow stamped himself upon it ... His prosperity has blossomed out with exquisitely ornate decoration. A band of carving runs along the front of the house, and from the curved stem of it branch out a hundred charming details, leaves, tendrils, strange flowers, human heads, Tudor roses, a crowned king and queen lying hand in hand, a baby, diving with a kick of fat legs into the bowl of an arum lily; and in the midst the merchant's mark upon a shield and the initials of the master of the house.

In this good taste of Paycocke the early capitalist we may perhaps see an instance of the difference between his day and ours. The merchant who grows suddenly enormously rich today, would he build himself a similarly beautiful home? The ornateness would almost certainly be there; but might it not more likely be cheap and flashy and ill-made?

The grace and charm of Paycocke's house, however, are not only due to the good taste of its owner. They are due no less (and perhaps even more) to the workmen who built it. Theirs was the age of fine craftsmanship, before the machine had cheapened their material or debased their cunning. Each one was an individualist. Each one was at liberty, within the limitations and discipline of the general design, to give free play to his talent. The same highly skilled craftsmen who, working in wood and stone, brick and flint, made the 'Wool' churches themselves such miracles of beauty, filling every nook and cranny with something to delight the eye and inspire the spirit, made also Paycocke's house; and there is a record of our social history in both of them.

Here, then, is where, sometime late in the second half of the fifteenth century, Thomas Paycocke brought his young bride. But Margaret was not destined to enjoy her new home for very long. Nor did she bear her husband any children. And soon after she died, we find Thomas taking to himself a second wife, one Anne Cotton. She, it is true, bore him the son he was longing for; but he died a little while before the child was born. So, for all his wealth and for all his influential connections up and down the land, Thomas may yet have been a lonely man in the house he was so proud of.

Out in the village, and indeed in all the surrounding countryside, he was certainly loved and much respected. We can gather this much from his Will.

Most Wills of rich men in those days were lengthy and ran to enormous detail. Indeed Thomas Paycocke's is a quite extraordinary document. He seems to have forgotten nobody, from the great Abbey a mile behind his house, where he must often have attended Mass and with whose Abbot, no doubt, he was on friendly terms to the humble apprentices who learned their trade at his looms.

It is well worth while setting forth in detail some of the items in the Will, for if something of Thomas Paycocke comes alive again for us in his house, even more of him comes alive in his Will.

There are bequests for Humphrey Stoner, 'some tyme my prentis' and for several of the Goodday family who were shearmen or cloth finishers. To John Beycham, who was a weaver, and to Robert Taylor, who was a fuller, both obviously in his employment, he not only left money but forgave them their debts to him, which suggests the best possible relationship between master and men.

Indeed, sections of the entire community that served him, in its various capacities within the industry, seem to have been remembered. 'I bequeth to all my Wevers, ffullers and Shermen that be not rehersed by name ii js iiijd apece. Item, I bequethe to be distributed amonge my Kembers, Carders and Spynners summa iiij li.' From these and other similar bequests it seems clear that Thomas Paycocke was very alive to the responsibilities inherent in his position as master and capitalist, which could not be said of all his fellow Clothiers at that time.

He was not only mindful of them individually but also collectively, as members of the village community in which he occupied so high a role. He left money, for instance, for the mending of their roads. As we know, roads throughout the kingdom then were in a deplorable state, and the heavy clay of Essex must have caused them to be particularly bad in the Coggeshall district. To mend matters somewhat, therefore, Thomas Paycocke decreed in his Will that of the forty pound which he bequeathed to Coggeshall itself, twenty pounds was to be spent on the upkeep of West Street (wherein his house stood) and the other twenty was 'to be layde on the fowle wayes bitwene Coxhall (Coggeshall) and Blackwater where as moost nede ys.' There were also bequests of money to be spent on roads further afield.

Exactly how much those items in his Will which mention Coggeshall Church and Abbey go to prove that he was religious above the usual run of such men it would be hard to say, since such bequests (though not necessarily so many or so liberal) fit into the social framework of a day when, before the Reformation, every man's life revolved around the Church, his obligations towards it being as strict as they were considerable.

Nevertheless, it would be very petty to read into these parts of Thomas Paycocke's Will no more than a bounden duty. He founded a Chantry in the church, desiring especially that it should be for the souls of himself, his wife, his father and mother, and his father-in-law, Thomas Harrold of Clare. He left money to found a charity which was to be given to six poor men who attended Mass there three times a week. He left five pounds to the Crutched Friars of Colchester to pray for him; and money also to the Grey Friars of Colchester and the Friars of Maldon, Chelmsford and Sudbury to repair their houses; and twenty shillings to the Friars of Clare and 'a kade of red herying'[1] at Lent.

Similarly, the bells of the Abbey, whose sound over the fields must have been so familiar to him, were to be rung at his burial, and masses and dirges were to be said at the church in his memory, for all of which he left the necessary money.

Evidently Thomas Paycocke was a different sort of man and master from those other Clothiers up and down the country who, their employees complained, imposed unfair conditions upon them, having little or no regard for their welfare but only for their own purses. The workers, then as now, treasured their independence, such as it was, which was not much. Many said that they had been better off under the rule of the Guilds, which protected them in every trade and calling; but the Guilds had fallen into disuse and the workers were at the mercy of their masters who, they

---

[1]   Kade, or cade = barrel.

complained, often used them so harshly that, though they should work all the days of the week and long into the nights, they could not earn sufficient to pay for their decent wants.

Moreover, another system was coming into practice in various parts of the country which deprived them still further of their independence by compelling them to work at looms set up at the Clothier's own house instead of their own cottage homes – a forestalling of the early factories which were the cause of so much abuse in later centuries.

There is nothing to show, however, that such a system was being practised by Thomas Paycocke: for one thing, his house would hardly seem to have lent itself to the installation of sufficient looms to make the transition worth while. So perhaps we may assume that in Coggeshall at this time the cloth trade was still carried on according to the outwork system, to the contentment of the workers, and that Thomas Paycocke really was as good and considerate a master as his Will suggests.

He died in 1518. Little can he have imagined how soon the scheme of things would fall apart, and a new order be imposed on the country. In less than a quarter of a century the Abbey across the fields was sacked. In time, too, the trade upon which the Paycocke fortunes had been established shifted its focus from country to town, from cottage to factory. And during the last War the church itself, where Paycocke and all his workers worshipped and where he was buried, was bombed, the tower and much more being quite destroyed.

But his house still stands, a memorial to a forgotten way of life as well as to the man whose trade mark and initials are carved on its oaken beams.

William Harvey

OF THE two famous names associated with the village of Hempstead, in north-west Essex, one is a great deal more familiar than the other. This is perhaps natural, since the one belonged to a highwayman and the other to a physician. Yet there is no doubt which was the greater man; Dick Turpin, born at the village inn, or William Harvey, buried in the village church. There is no doubt, either, who was the more worthy of remembrance: Turpin, who robbed and stole and murdered; or Harvey, who discovered the circulation of the blood.

But the sensational man always steals the thunder; and, for all his genius and international fame, there was never anything sensational about William Harvey – 'honest little Doctor Harvey,' as one of his contemporaries called him. His was one of the greatest medical discoveries of all time; scholars all over Europe acknowledged their debt to him, and kings and noblemen counted themselves honoured by his company; yet he remained to the end humble and most self-effacing.

A lifelike bust of him stands in the Harvey Chapel, at Hempstead church. His long hair nestles on his shoulders, after the manner of his day; his wide brow is furrowed; his eyebrows gently raised, as if in perpetual surprise; his features strong and manly. The likeness is probably a reliable one, for the bust was executed by one of the master masons of the time, Edward Marshall. 'Here,' writes Geof-

frey Keynes, who made a detailed study of the several existing portraits (or supposed portraits) of the great Doctor,
'you have the authentic Harvey, looking at life as it really is,
honest, forthright, in the best sense of the word, *scientific.*'

What one does not get from this sculpture, however,
since it is a bust only, is the sense of the man's small stature,
about which several of his friends commented at the time.
For instance, Aubrey, the sage and gossip of Harvey's day,
who has left us so many word-portraits of his famous
contemporaries, says of Harvey: 'In person he was not tall,
but of the smallest stature; round faced, olivaster complexion' (a word then implying the hard colour of wainscot, an
imported wood, and often used as a description of men's
faces), 'little eyes, round, very black, full of spirits; his hair
black as a raven, but quite white twenty years before he
died.'

Hempstead is a quiet enough village even today: three
hundred years ago, when Harvey's body was brought there,
to rest in the family vault, it must certainly have been a great
deal more so. On that one day, however, as the enormous
procession bore the coffin up the road to the church, it was
no doubt lively enough: not often is such a scene witnessed
in so quiet a village. The procession had come all the way
from London, fifty miles distant, and it included some of
the most famous men of the time.

How the Hempstead folk must have stared! Villagers still
love a funeral – it breaks the monotony of the daily round.
Moreover, it is nearly always the funeral of somebody they
know very well, and, although they may merely hang round
the churchyard wall to watch, they feel a real concern and
sympathy: it is one of themselves who has come to the end
of his days.

On that midsummer day in 1657, when the important folk filed through the doorway into Hempstead church, no doubt there were even more villagers than usual staring over the wall; but they would scarcely have been feeling concern and sympathy, for William Harvey had never been a familiar figure among them. True, the family mansion (long since diminished) was off the main road through the village, and the family vault was in the church; but Harvey himself had spent most of his days either in London or abroad, in college and hospital and Court.

He was not even born in Hempstead, but in Kent; and he went to school at Canterbury Grammar School. Indeed, his closest contact with the place (Hempstead lies not many miles from the Cambridgeshire border) had probably been while he was a student at Gonville and Caius College, preparing for medicine and where, in 1597, he took his BA.

Caius College, Cambridge, had a bias, as it still has today, towards anatomical studies. In fact, one of the privileges accorded to the college was that of being allowed to appropriate annually the bodies of two criminals who had been executed in the town. These were used for dissecting purposes. At any rate, the young William Harvey early showed himself especially adept in anatomical research, and it may well have been that the bias of his college was largely responsible for the rapid development of his genius which ultimately led to such important discoveries.

From Cambridge, after he had taken his degree, Harvey made his slow way to Italy, where, in 1600, he entered the famous University of Padua. Here his chief teacher was the great Fabricus, the most eminent anatomist of his day in all Europe. That Harvey showed far more than usual ability there is evident, not only from the fact that in 1602 the degree of Doctor of Physic was conferred on him, but also and much more from the fact that the internationally renowned Fabricus bestowed upon him his friendship.

One of the features of Padua University was a great anatomical theatre which had only recently been erected as a tribute to Fabricus. It was circular in design, the galleries rising in tiers almost to the ceiling from the well of the building. The students stood behind high, carved railings of oak to watch the dissections being conducted at the centralised table below. The subjects for dissection were brought up through a trap-door. There were no windows in the place and the experiments were carried out solely by the aid of candlelight.

The use of candles, for such intricate and delicate work, is typical of the handicaps under which science was conducted in those days. Throughout his life, for instance, Harvey was aided in his tremendous discoveries by nothing more elaborate than a simple lens. One wonders what he might not have achieved if he could have had access to the marvellous equipment which today is at the disposal of any student. But it is often the way with genius that the very handicaps act as a spur to eventual triumphs.

Harvey was only twenty-four years old when he was made a Doctor of Medicine. Two years later, when he was back again in England, he was admitted to the College of Physicians. Soon afterwards he married Elizabeth, daughter of Dr Launcelot Browne, who was Physician in turn to Queen Elizabeth and King James I.

Almost all we know of Harvey's wife is that she was 'tall, of a dark complexion and somewhat severe aspect' – not a very endearing portrait. We also know that she kept a parrot. In one of his works Harvey had something to say about this parrot, and it is worth quoting not only because it throws a tiny light on the domestic scene in Harvey's home, but also because it provides an instance of the way in which the learned man loved to draw his examples and illustrations from the everyday scene about him. Here is what he says:–

A parrot, a handsome bird and a famous talker, had long been a pet of my wife's. It was so tame that it wandered freely through the house, called for its mistress when she was abroad, greeted her cheerfully when it found her, answered her call, flew to her, and aiding himself with beak and claws climbed up her dress to her shoulder, where it walked down her arm and after settled upon her hand ... I believed all this to proceed from its usual familiarity and love of being noticed, for I always looked upon the creature as a male, on account of its skill in talking and singing ... until, not long after the carressings mentioned, the parrot, which had lived for so many years in health, fell ill, and by and by being seized with repeated attacks of convulsions, died, to our great sorrow, in its Mistress's lap, where it had so often loved to lie. On making a post-mortem examination to discover the cause of death I found an almost complete egg in its oviduct, but it was addled.

Young as he still was, Harvey was already making a considerable reputation for himself, so that it surprised nobody when, three years after his marriage, in 1607, he was elected a Fellow of the College of Physicians and almost immediately offered the post of Physician to St Batholomew's Hospital. In addition, there was his private practice, a considerable one which included Lord Chancellor Bacon; yet all the time he persisted in his research work, making dissections and observations upon all manner of animals and insects, from dogs, pigs, serpents, slugs, fishes, oysters, to chicks while still in the shell. Relentlessly Harvey pursued his search for scientific truth.

And then, in 1615, at the age of thirty-six, he was appointed Lumleian lecturer in the College of Physicians. His original notes for the lectures which he gave (on anatomy and surgery) have somehow survived. They are written in a crabbed, atrocious hand, on both sides of about a hundred small slips of paper, and they include eleven rules which he laid down for himself when delivering lectures. Of these rules the following is typical as showing the wise and generous attitude of the true scholar: 'Not to praise or dispraise other anatomists, for all did well, and there was some excuse for those who are in error.' Incidentally, the little whalebone pointer, tipped with silver, which he used at his lectures, is still one of the most treasured possessions of the Royal College.

The picture of William Harvey which we can piece together, a fragment here and a fragment there, is altogether attractive. Quiet and gentle, he was the genuine scholar, absorbed only in the work for which he lived. A true humility often accompanies greatness, and Harvey was a fine example of this. Although he was still comparatively young, famous men already acknowledged his worth, but he shied away from fame and publicity of all kinds; and when his duties allowed, he liked nothing better than to ponder over the poems of Virgil, his favourite author.

He could have become, had he so cared, a very wealthy man; but his mind was set on other things than money. He was one of seven brothers, five of whom, as merchants in the City of London, accumulated great riches: he alone, among them, showed no interest in financial matters. In fact, his affairs were managed for him by his brother Eliab.

His shyness and humility were perhaps most evident in the reluctance with which he made his great discovery public. Indeed, he showed such unwillingness to thrust his revolutionary views on the world that it was not until twelve years after he had actually made his discovery of the circulation of the blood that he allowed his book on the subject to be published. He even seemed indifferent as to whether his views were published or not: his one concern was with the furthering of scientific truth. 'The crowd of foolish scribblers,' he wrote, 'is scarcely less than the swarms of flies in the height of summer, and threatens with their crude and flimsy productions to stifle us as with smoke.'

De Motu Cordis, as his book was called, was finally published, in 1628, in Frankfurt, which was then the great book market of Europe. It consisted of seventy-two pages only; yet it proved to be among the most important medical books ever written, if not actually the most important.

One of the first theories put forward in explanation of the action of the blood had been evolved by Aristotle, who held that the blood, elaborated from the food in the liver, was carried to the heart and thence distributed over the body by the veins. Later, it came to be held, in addition, that, while the veins carried the blood from the heart to the members of the body, the arteries carried a subtle kind of air or spirit. Nobody seems to have thought of the blood as working in a continuous stream, circulating through the body and returning to its source: rather it was supposed to be slow and irregular in direction 'like the circulation of air in a house.'

There was, in fact, no notion until Harvey came on the scene that the heart was the motor power governing the movement of the blood. It was Harvey's contention, based on the observation of life itself and not upon the words and theories of his predecessors, that the blood in the right ventricle of the heart is sent to the lungs and round by the pulmonary artery to the left ventricle, and that the blood in the left ventricle is again sent into the arteries, round by the smaller veins, to the right ventricle – a complete circulation.

'The heart, consequently, is the beginning of life,' Harvey wrote, 'the sun of the microcosm, even as the sun in his turn might well be designated the heart of the world; for it is the heart by whose virtue and pulse the blood is moved, made apt to nourish, and is preserved from corruption and coagulation.'

'A motion, as it were, in a circle' – that, in brief, is the substance of Harvey's discovery of the circulation of the blood. It sounds familiar enough today; but in 1628, when it was announced to the world, it was revolutionary and caused, inevitably, a tremendous stir in the medical and scientific world.

Aubrey said that after the publication of *De Motu Cordis* Harvey 'fell mightily in his practice; 'twas believed by the vulgar that he was crack-brained, and all the physicians were against him.' But this is almost certainly an exaggeration, at least in so far as learned physicians were concerned: with one or two exceptions these acknowledged the theory as proven and indisputable.

In any case, Harvey, already used to attack and abuse for his innovations in medical science, took little heed of his critics and mostly refused to argue with them. He stood secure in his convictions without need either of approval or of correction. Such criticism as there was, came mainly from the Continent: at home his fame grew abundantly. In 1631 he was appointed Physician to King Charles I, accompanying him on his tour to Scotland when he went to Holyrood to be crowned. Indeed, his standing at Court shows well enough in what honour he was held; but he remained at heart the same quiet, unassuming man he had always been, a student before everything else.

Among his friends at Court was the Earl of Arundel. It happened one day that the Earl heard of a man living in Shropshire who was reputed to be one hundred and fifty-two years old. His name was Thomas Parr. Though now greatly impaired in health, his sight gone, his memory failing, Parr nevertheless was still a remarkable man for his age. In his one hundred and thirtieth year he had continued to earn his living as an agricultural labourer, even to the extent of being able to thresh corn (with the flail). Lord Arundel decided to bring this astonishing ancient to London in order to show him to the King. Not surprisingly, the contrast from rural peace to city noise, from peasant frugality to plenty, proved too much for him at such an age, so that he died.

To one absorbed in the study of physiology, as Harvey was, Thomas Parr would of course be a source of considerable interest; and so it is not surprising that on the old man's death Harvey was called in to conduct the post-mortem. His report was worded in the same exact and factual manner he always used in his medical studies; and, incidentally, it throws a certain light on the London of his time.

After a description of the various organs of the body, as he found them, Harvey continues:- 'The cause of death seemed fairly referrible to a sudden change in the non-naturals, the chief mischief being connected with the change of air, which through the whole course of life had been inhaled in perfect purity - light, cool and mobile, whereby the praecordia and lungs were more freely ventilated and cooled; but in this great advantage, in this grand cherisher of life this city is especially destitute; a city whose grand characteristic is an immense concourse of men and animals, and where ditches abound, and filth of offal lie scattered about, to say nothing of the smoke engendered by the general use of sulphurous coal as fuel, whereby the air is at all times rendered heavy, but much more so in the autumn than at any other season. Such an atmosphere could not have been found otherwise than insalubrious to one coming from the open, sunny and healthy region of Salop; it must have been especially so to one already aged and infirm.

'And then for one hitherto used to live on food unvaried in kind, and very simple in its nature, to be set at a table loaded with variety of viands, and tempted not only to eat more than wont, but to partake of strong drink, it must needs fall out that the functions of all the natural organs would become deranged. Whence the stomach at length failing, and the excretions long retained, the work of concoction proceeding languidly, the liver getting loaded, the blood stagnating in the veins, the spirits frozen, the heart, the source of life, oppressed, the lungs obstructed and made impervious to the ambient air, the gradual habit rendered more compact, so that it could no longer exhale or perspire – no wonder that the soul, little content with such a prison, took its flight.'

In 1642, Parliament took up arms against the King and now the gentle, unwarlike Harvey suddenly found himself, as King's Physician and Court attendant, in the thick of trouble. The Parliamentarians broke into his lodgings, stole his furniture, and, what was far worse, destroyed his books, including his notes and all the material for a treatise he was preparing on the generation of insects. Aubrey said this was 'the greatest crucifying to him that ever he had in all his life,' and for once his words could hardly have been an exaggeration of the case.

It was Aubrey, too, who left us a vivid little description of Harvey's unmartial behaviour at the Battle of Edgehill.

> When Charles I by reason of the tumults left London he (Harvey) attended him and was at the fight of Edgehill with him; and during the fight the Prince and Duke of York (they were children at the time) were committed to his care; he told me that he with-drew with them under a hedge and took out of his pocket a book and read; but he had not read very long before a bullet of a great gun grazed on the ground near him, which made him remove his station.

Whether this well-known and often quoted incident is true or not, it is of a character that would certainly have been in keeping with the 'honest little Doctor.'

With the King, Harvey remained in Oxford, where he was made Warden of Merton College, until 1646, when the town finally surrendered to the Parliamentary forces and both Charles and Harvey returned to London.

Harvey was now sixty-nine, too old, no doubt he thought, as the twinges of gout grew more and more painful, to take up his practice again. But not too old to continue with his studies. Henceforth, he decided, these should be his sole concern: he would enjoy, unhindered at last, the scholar's solitude and peace he had always preferred but not always been allowed. The country was in a confused and sorry state; his royal master had been beheaded; what but his studies remained?

I found him (wrote his friend Dr Ent, in 1650) Democritus-like, his countenance cheerful, his mind serene, embracing all within its sphere. I forthwith saluted him and asked if all were well with him? 'How can it be?' said he, 'whilst the Commonwealth is full of distractions, and I myself am still in the open sea? And truly,' he continued, 'did I not find solace in my studies, and a balm for my spirit in the memory of my observations of former years, I should feel little desire for longer life. But so it has been, that this life of obscurity, this vacation from public business, which causes tedium and disgust to so many, has proved a sovereign remedy to me.'

Just as Harvey had been reluctant to publish his former work, the great *De Motu Cordis*, so now he showed a similar reluctance to give the world his latest book on the generation of animals, *De Generatione Animalium*. 'Much better is it oftentimes,' he said, 'to grow wise at home and in private, than by publishing what you have amassed with infinite labour, to stir up tempers that may rob you of peace and quiet for the rest of your days.'

Nevertheless, he did publish the book; and when it appeared, it proved to be as long as the other book had been short and to have nothing revolutionary about it. Nor did it contribute much towards the solution of the mystery of how life begins.

Like the first book, however, it was all based on first-hand evidence (he incubated eggs in his room at Oxford and had the King's special permission to dissect deer from Windsor Park) and it was full of the same kind of close and revealing description, as the following example bears witness:–

> ... There are some who, in hunting, when there are some forty hounds upon the trace of the game and all are giving tongue together, will nevertheless, and from a distance, tell which dog is at the head of the pack, which at the tail, which chases on the hot scent, which is running off at fault; whether the game is still running or is at bay; whether the stag has run far, or has but just been raised from his lair. And all this amid the din of dogs, and men, and horns, and surrounded by an unknown and gloomy wood.

Harvey was in his seventy-third year when *De Generatione Animalium* was published and mindful of the fact that his end could not now be far off. Much has been made of certain eccentricities which he showed in these last years, but they are harmless enough and even endearing. His great-niece, for instance, told how 'he used to walk out in a morning, combing his hair in the fields.' His salt-cellar was always filled with sugar, which he ate instead of salt. 'He was humoursome and would sit down exactly at the time he had appointed whether the company was come or not.'

Aubrey, of course, adds his quota to these innocent anecdotes.

He was much and often troubled (he writes) with the gout and his way of cure was thus: He would sit with his legs bare, though it were frost, on the leads of Cockaine House (his brother's home), put them into a pail of water till he was almost dead with cold, then betake himself to his stove, and so 'twas gone. Or again, Aubrey continues, He did delight to be in the dark, and told me he could then best contemplate ... whilst at the house at Combe in Surrey, he had caves made in the ground in which he delighted in summer-time to meditate.

To the end, however, Harvey's mind remained as lucid as ever, and it would seem that in spite of everything he was tolerably happy.

He died in the house of his brother Eliab, at Rochampton, of a stroke, on June 3rd, 1657, in his seventy-ninth year. 'The morning of his death about ten o'clock he went to speak and found he had the dead palsey in his tongue.'

His Will, written a few years previously and in his own hand, is an elaborate and revealing document. He was as exact in enumerating his bequests as if he were detailing scientific observations. His family, his friends, his servants, all were remembered. To the College of Physicians, with which he had been so closely associated, he gave 'all my bookes and papers and my best Persia long Carpet and my blue sattin imbroyedred Cushion one paire of brasse Andi-

rons with fire-shovell and tongues of brasse for the orna-
ment of the meeting roome I have erected for that purpose.'
To his friend Dr Ent he gave 'all the presses and shelves he
please to make use of and five pounds to buy him a ring to
keepe and weare in remembrance of me,' whilst to another
friend, Dr Scarbough, he gave 'all my little silver instru-
ments of surgerie.'

John Ray

I T WOULD have been very unlikely, three hundred years ago, that any poor village lad, however clever, would get to a university, not only because there were no scholarships in the sense in which we understand them today, but also because, in those very class-conscious days, a good education was still the privilege of the few.

Yet in 1644, John Ray, who was the son of a blacksmith in the little village of Black Notley, not far from Braintree, in Essex, was admitted to Trinity College, Cambridge.

Ray was then in his sixteenth year, and the only schooling he had so far received was at Braintree, where he attended a school which was really a converted chapel in the parish church. (Incidentally, on one of the stone pillars by the entrance to the chapel there are still some marks which look as if they might have been made by the boys in sharpening their slate pencils, and John Ray's mark may well be one of them.) Not only did this village blacksmith's son manage to get into Trinity College, but he did so well when he was there that he eventually became a Fellow and remained at the College for eighteen years – one of its most famous scholars. His subject was natural history.

In fact, right from the start John Ray must have been unusually clever. We know next to nothing about his boyhood, except that the Vicar of Braintree at that time happened to be a very learned man and it was almost certainly due to him that Ray went up to the University.

Something was probably due, also, to his parents, not because they were at all clever, but because they were obviously country folk of the finest character. His father was a good craftsman, occupying quite an important place in the life of that little village community, and his mother was a staunch, religious woman who, we are told, looked after the sick and was a friend to the poor cottagers in their times of trouble.

The blacksmith's forge still stands, complete with bellows and anvil, but it is disused today and boys no longer hang about in the quiet, green lane watching the sparks fly in the dim interior. Close by, too, there is still the timber and plaster house where the blacksmith lived with his family. Nor has the village itself changed very much since those days, for Black Notley lies well off the main routes.

And not far off, through the trees, is the church where John Ray was baptized and where, as boy and man, he worshipped. To the east of the porch, in the church-yard, an elaborate tomb may be seen among the lichened gravestones. It marks the burial place of the one-time blacksmith's son, and a long inscription in Latin tells his story.

What was John Ray's story? How did it happen that this child of humble village parents attained such fame that his name was known all over the civilised world? And what reason have we today to remember him with pleasure and gratitude?

Almost everybody nowadays is interested in natural history in one form or another. Never were there so many bird-watchers, flower-hunters, insect-collectors as there are in Britain today. We study wild birds for pleasure, often giving up much time and going to a great deal of trouble to do so. We look out for wild flowers, as they appear in their season, and keep careful notes of where they grow, what they are like, and when we found them. Insects, too, in their thousands, from bees to spiders, from ants to glow-worms, hold such a fascination for us that we want to know all we possibly can about them.

Hundred of books are published to satisfy our curiosity by helping us to identify the birds, beasts and flowers of our island and to inform us of their structure, behaviours, and way of life. Soon, it would seem, we shall know all there is to know about them. The study of them is everybody's hobby today. And yet, three hundred years ago, when John Ray was a boy, even learned scholars knew very little about them, and much of what they thought they knew was quite inaccurate.

Students of natural history, then, thought that swallows disappeared in winter into ponds and lakes. They thought that 'cuckoo spittle' was rained down from the skies, like manna. They thought that the dung of peacocks was a certain cure for head-aches. Indeed, a lot of their so-called science was no more than superstition. They did not so much observe as guess.

And this was just where John Ray was different from the rest. He saw the existing confusion in the natural history of his day and he turned it to order. He substituted direct, first-hand observation for mere guesswork and exact science for superstition. He sifted the work of all who had preceded him, the good from the bad, the false from the true. The facts, thus proven, he added to his own studies, thereby laying the foundations upon which all future natural history was to be based.

John Ray was, in short, the father of natural history as we understand it today.

The story of so remarkable a man is obviously worth looking into closely. The trouble is that so little is known about him. He told us next to nothing about himself, and others have not told us much more. It is as though John Ray wished to live only in his work. He was immensely industrious and wrote between twenty and thirty books. It might be supposed that these would tell us all we want to know about him; but in fact they tell us very little except what we can read between the lines. Like the fine scholar he was, he never allowed himself to come between his reader and the subject-matter on hand: in his books he hid his personality completely.

And there was another reason why we are today so much in the dark about him. After the academic fashion of the time, he wrote in Latin, which was the student's international language. The effect was that for many years he remained the exclusive property of the few. The man in the street never heard of him. Even when, nearer our own time, natural history became a matter of increasing interest to the general public, John Ray's name remained largely unknown outside academic circles.

But at last he has begun to occupy the popular place he deserves; and this he owes to another Cambridge scholar, Dr C E Raven, who, in 1942, after many years of devoted research, published a study of Ray's life and work which future scholars will scarcely be able to improve upon. Dr Raven has examined every possible source of information, from Ray's own words to the words of those who knew him or were influenced by him; and if it still remains true that little is known, enough has now come to light to transform the shadow into a real man. And what is more, it is clear now that every one of us today who takes an interest, however amateurly, in bird, beast or flower, owes an immeasurable debt to the blacksmith's son of Black Notley.

Hitherto it has always been claimed, in popular opinion, that Gilbert White of Selborne was the father of English natural history. All the limelight was focussed on this Hampshire village clergyman and scholar who lived nearly a hundred years later than Ray. Yet the truth is that White could scarcely have written his one famous book, *The Natural History and Antiquities of Selborne* (1789), if Ray had not preceded him and prepared the way. No doubt White was aware of this, though he acknowledged his debt no further than to speak of 'the excellent Mr Ray.'

Of the two, Ray's was certainly the more original mind, the more perceptive eye. Nor did he enjoy any of the Hampshire clergyman's advantages, either as boy or man. White came of a noble family; he grew up in a cultured home; and, as a bachelor clergyman in a quiet village he had leisure and a regular and sufficient income. Ray, on the other hand, was hounded by poverty all his life. His humble parentage must have stood in his way at Cambridge. And when he had left Cambridge behind him and had settled down in his native village, he had only the barest minimum of money on which to keep his wife and family.

Moreover, Ray was a sick man for many years. He was driven to write by poverty as well as by a passionate desire to get at the truth. Leisure he never knew, nor wanted: all he asked was strength enough to do his work. 'I thank God,' he wrote, 'that I am able to go on with this work, though I have little or no intermission of pain.' And even on his death-bed he was planning a new book on insects.

But let us, in the light of Dr Raven's searching studies, look a little closer at this remarkable man.

When he went up to Cambridge, from what he himself called 'our paltry county school at Braintree,' he probably already knew a certain amount of Latin. Latin, in fact, was expected of all educated persons. But, as the boy sharpened his pencil on the school wall, did his teacher guess how soon he would become so proficient that Latin flowed from his pen as fluently (and conversationally) as if it were his native tongue? And not only did he master Latin, but also Greek and Hebrew, French and Italian, so that he could read what past authorities all over the civilised world had written on his favourite subject and could communicate with the living authorities in their own language. All this was to be of the greatest use to him when he finally decided to make the study of natural history his life's work.

But he did not come to such a decision for some time. In fact, the first book he wrote, whilst at Cambridge, was a *Collection of English Proverbs.* Not for nothing had he stood in the doorway of his father's forge and listened to the talk of the rough Essex carters and farm-hands who brought their masters' horses to be shod. His quick ear missed nothing of what they said; and his quick mind seized upon the homespun proverbs and local sayings with which their conversation was so liberally sprinkled.

This first little book, however, though it is amusing enough today for the light it throws on country thought and manners long ago, was no more than a trifle and gave no hint whatever of the real work that was to follow.

Indeed, Ray's first important book did not appear until 1659, when he had been in residence for fifteen years. It was called *Catalogus Cantabryiam* and was a list of the Cambridgeshire plants he had himself seen and studied. Its real importance lay in the fact that it was the first local

Flora, or wild flower book, showing where to look for the flowers of a particular locality and how to identify them when found. Nowadays, every county, every region, has its own *Flora,* which the flower-lover should immediately get hold of when he goes to study the flowers of any special region. But in Ray's day such guides did not exist.

The *Cambridge Catalogue* started him along the road he was to follow for the rest of his life. Not that natural history was his only interest. He continued to study languages, and his deeply religious character compelled him from time to time to write religious books.

But it was to his study of all wild life, and of botany in particular, that his greatest powers were to be given. There is a passage in the introduction to *Cambridge Catalogue* which tells how almost by accident, this came about. 'I had been ill,' he wrote, 'physically and mentally, and had to rest from more serious study and ride or walk. There was leisure to contemplate by the way what lay constantly before the eyes and were so often trodden thoughtlessly under foot, the varying beauty of plants, the cunning craftsmanship of nature. First the rich array of Springtime meadows, then the shape, colour and structure of particular plants fascinated and absorbed me: interest in botany became a passion.'

Ray was rather laughed at for the zeal he showed in studying the plants of Cambridgeshire. But one or two friends caught his enthusiasm and together they would tramp about the country, and even into the Fens, searching for plants and identifying them. Nothing was included in Ray's list of plants that he did not actually find, and some he even studied in detail in a little garden he cultivated outside his college rooms.

This first-hand way of studying plants was something quite new, and it was not long before others began to see the importance of Ray's approach. One person in particular saw the value of what was being done and gave all the help he could. His name was Francis Willoughby, and he was Ray's first pupil as a College tutor. Willoughby soon became friend as well as pupil, and for several years – until Willoughby's death, in fact – the two worked closely together in this exciting new study. Willoughby's friendship was a great advantage to Ray, not only because the younger man's vitality acted as a spur to his inherent caution, but also because Willoughby was a wealthy young man and well able to finance Ray in important expeditions, both at home and abroad, which otherwise he could not have afforded.

The Cambridge years were as happy as they were industrious; but unfortunately they did not last. They might have lasted if Ray had cared to be false to his conscience, but this was something he could never allow.

To understand what happened it is necessary to look briefly at the state of affairs in England at this time. The Restoration of 1660 not only restored King and Parliament, it also restored the Bishops and the Prayer Book and the Anglican form of worship. The new order was imposed by an Act of Uniformity, in 1662, whereby King Charles broke his promise to grant freedom of conscience to everybody. The clergy who would not conform were, instead, deprived of their livings. It had been a condition of Ray's Fellowship at Trinity that he should be ordained, and so he came under the Act. Admittedly he was neither Presbyterian nor Independent; but he did dislike ritual, and to that extent at least he was sympathetic to the Puritans. But the real trouble was that religion, for him, was essentially a personal matter, and it offended his conscience to have religion made a condition of employment. He therefore saw no alternative but to refuse to comply with the Act ('I cannot do it,' he said; 'whatever happens, I cannot do it') and, by so doing, to give up his post at Cambridge. Liberty, he said is 'a sweet thing,' and he showed now that he was willing to pay the highest possible price for it. The College implored him to stay on, and he might easily have done so, for these things, then as now, can sometimes be 'arranged.' But Ray listened only to the voice of his conscience.

So it came about, most ironically, that he, who took no part whatever in politics, being entirely absorbed in his work, was by politics driven from a position of security and affluence into one of poverty. From the happy conditions of Cambridge he retired, for conscience' sake, to the little Essex backwater of Black Notley.

It must have been a hard decision. In the University he was financially secure: he held a position of importance: he could work under conditions that were ideal for the scholar: and he had the satisfaction of training pupils to carry on with his work. There was, too, another matter. Ever since his father died, his mother, whom he greatly loved, had been entirely dependent upon him. He had built a house for her at Black Notley, called Dewlands, and here she was living at his expense. He must have wondered how, deprived of his income and dependent now on what he could earn by his writing, he would in future be able to honour his obligation.

At the same time, it is possible that, even in the midst of his worry, he may have seen that the course he had decided upon would have certain advantages to help redress the balance.

He would he poor; but he would he free.

He would have no other calls now upon his time and energy: he could devote himself completely henceforth to the work which all his Cambridge years had been leading up to. And anyhow he was still only thirty-five years old, in his prime and at the top of his power; in spite of all, he could face his life's work with sure confidence.

For a concise summing-up of what that life's work was to be one cannot possibly do better than quote Dr Raven. Here is what he says in his detailed study of John Ray:

> His greatness is that in a time of transition and universal turmoil he saw the need for precise and ordered knowledge, set himself to test the old and explore the new, and by dint of immense labour in the field and in the study laid the foundations of modern science in many branches of zoology and botany. He studied, corrected, and collated the existing literature; he collected, identified, investigated, described and classified mammals, crytogams (i.e., plants without flowers, such as mosses, lichens, ferns, etc.), and all known plants; he contributed richly to the advance of geology and made observations in astronomy and physics; he was a pioneer in the study of language and first revealed the importance of dialect and folk-speech; he did as much as any man of his time to develop a new understanding and interpretation of religion; more perhaps than any man he enabled the transition from the mediæval to the modern outlook. That he could do so is due not only to his own genius and opportunities, but to the character of his inheritance and the circumstances of his upbringing.

It is a formidable accomplishment for any man: for a village blacksmith's son in the seventeenth century it almost amounts to the miraculous.

From 1662, when Ray forfeited his Fellowship under the Act of Uniformity he had fifty-three more years to live. Not all of these were spent at Black Notley. First there were some years of travel, all over Britain and abroad, and mostly in the company (and possibly at the expense) of his wealthy young friend Francis Willoughby. There seems to have been scarcely any part of Great Britain he did not visit; and the aim and intention of his travels was to gather material for an extended British Flora after the manner of his local Cambridge Flora.

It was the whole point of Ray's study of botany that he took nothing for granted: he must go and see everything for himself. What the old herbalists had already written might sometimes be useful to him, but it could never be relied upon.

In those days of bad roads and inadequate means of communication it was no simple task to travel all over Britain, penetrating even into the remotest parts, anywhere, in fact, where he might expect to find the particular plants he was in search of. Willoughby, with his enthusiasm and youthful vitality, proved a good companion. And Ray himself, moreover, had a lively eye for other things than flowers. We gather, in fact, from all manner of sources, that he was a most friendly man, at home equally with rich and poor, interested in everything he saw.

Ray's botanical notes, therefore, were often interspersed with observations upon old churches, people, local customs and manners. 'At the time we were in Scotland,' (he wrote) 'divers women were burnt for witches, they reported, to the number of about one hundred and thirty.' Or again, he noted that in Lincoln 'the choristers had no surplices but only gowns with capes faced with lambskin.' The famous water of Harrogate

> 'though it be pellucid enough, yet stinks noisomely like rotten eggs.' As for the Scots, 'they cannot endure to hear their country or countrymen spoken against. They have neither good bread, cheese or drink. They cannot make them, nor will they learn. Their butter is very indifferent, and one would wonder how they could contrive to make it so bad.'

But first and foremost in his travels, of course, it was plants that he was after; and when finally his *English Catalogue* was published, it proved to be the most detailed and authoritative list of plants (and the localities where they were to be found) that had ever appeared; and although, today, many of the plants he listed have disappeared from the places where Ray and Willoughby found them, the *Catalogue* remains a useful and informative students' guide.

After his travels, Ray lived for a while at Middleton Hall, Willoughby's country seat in Warwickshire. Here the friends studied the specimens they had brought back with them. But Ray was not destined to enjoy the liberty of Middleton Hall any more than he had been destined to enjoy the security of Trinity College. One day in May, 1672, while he was at work in the great library, alone, news was brought to him that his friend Willoughby was dead. Ray was grief-stricken. 'Give us grace,' he prayed 'to imitate his eminent graces and virtues'; and he made it his mission henceforth, come what might, to supervise the education of Willoughby's two young children and to prepare for publication the mass of natural history notes which he had left behind.

Willoughby bequeathed his old friend an annuity of £70, which, of course, was worth a good deal more then than it would be now. Indeed, frugal as Ray was, wanting money only in so far as it enabled him to do his work, he retired on his annuity to Black Notley in circumstances, as he said, 'though not splendid nor affluent, yet ... tolerable enough not to say easy to me.' This money, together with the small sums that came to him from his several books, constituted his entire income for the remaining twenty-five years of his life.

Fresh travel, of course, was now out of the question; but he had already accumulated all he needed, in notes and knowledge, to form the basis for all his future work. As for contact with other great minds, the botanical scholars of the world must now come to him, since he could not go to them.

Ray's world, in fact, was now narrowed down to the little Essex village where he was born. Comparative poverty and increasing ill-health chained him to the fields and lanes of home. But he was no prisoner. Indeed, the miracle was that here, in this remote and simple place, he found so much to study – flowers, birds, fish, insects – that even twenty-five years was not long enough to turn it all to account in his books, so that when death finally came he was busy preparing a book on insects.

'Give me always the same, plain road,' Richard Jefferies, a much later naturalist, was to exclaim, knowing that however long he lived he would never see all there was to

see, know all there was to know, about even such an ordinary place as the lane outside his house.

And so it was with John Ray. He had travelled far and
wide. He had enjoyed the society and friendship of learned
men. He had lived in the cultured ease of mansion and
college. And now it had all come down to this, the homely
fields and simple people of a tiny Essex village. But it would
be enough. He had the 'seeing eye' and the trained, enquir-
ing mind; and the small compass of Black Notley would
provide all the material he required for his great work.

A year after Willoughby died, Ray married Margaret
Oakeley, the twenty years old daughter of an Oxfordshire
gentleman. If little is known about Ray, much less is known
about his wife. More than twice her age, he seems to have
had doubts as to whether he was justified in asking her to
share his life. Two little notes in Ray's handwriting suggest
that this was so. 'You were brought up in a different way,'
reads one of them, 'and not likely to love my prayers.' And
the other expresses his fear that, if he should have children,
they 'will never delight in my company for that I shall be old
before they come to years of discretion.' But his fears were
apparently groundless. At any rate, there is nothing to show
that Margaret ever thought other than well of her husband's
devotion to religion; and the children, when they came, so
far from not delighting in their father's company, even ran
to help him, catching butterflies for him to examine and
flowers in the fields for him to identify.

Yet the first years, at least, could not have been easy for
Margaret, for the Rays had not even a home of their own.
They had to wait six years for one. In 1679 Ray's mother
died, and John and Margaret moved into Dewlands. The
house was a small one, little larger, in fact, than the cottage

beside the smithy. A big central hall, with a great open fireplace, provided the living-room. There was a bakehouse and also a brewhouse. Ray's special room was a small one off the hall, where he housed his library, studied his botanical specimens, and wrote his books.

Dewlands stood until 1900 when it was burned down and a new house built on the site.

As for the young wife, whose first and only home it was, she seems to have been a sensible, practical woman, who, if she understood very little of her husband's work, cared for him and contentedly busied herself about the house. She needed to be a careful housewife, for Ray never made much money by his books, important though they were, and prices (sugar at 4d [2 pence] a pound and candles at 5½d [nearly 3 pence]) were rising. And when the children came, it must have been even more difficult to make ends meet.

Ray himself needed to be busy with his work, for certainly there was not much congenial company for him in the neighbourhood. Aubrey, the invaluable social commentator of the day, said of Black Notley that it was 'barren of wits, here being but few of the gentry or clergy who mind anything that is ingenious.' It seems that the most congenial person Ray found in the village was a retired grocer from Braintree, one James Coker. In Braintree itself, however, the position was not too bad. The town lay on the main thoroughfare from Suffolk and Norfolk into London, and the rattling stage-coaches kept it fairly closely in touch with the world outside. Then, as now, Braintree was a centre of the prosperous cloth-trade; and its prosperity attracted to the town men of good standing and lively intelligence, especially among the clergy and doctors. There was one doctor in particular, Samuel Dale, who became so infected with Ray's enthusiasm that he even helped him in his botanical studies and in time somewhat took the place of Willoughby.

Increasingly, however, as the years passed, Ray became more and more reliant upon the post. Letters from fellow scholars in various parts of the world stood him in stead of talk. The advice and help of 'the great Mr Ray,' as he was hailed all over Europe, was sought by scholars everywhere; and by his correspondence with them he spread his theory of natural history far and wide.

The village carrier, with his covered cart, played his humble part in the great man's work. He would collect parcels of specimens from the stage-coach and carry them home to Black Notley along with the villagers' goods which they had commissioned him to buy in Braintree. The arrival of the carrier at Dewlands must have been one of the most important events in the Ray family's quiet days. And not only did he bring parcels of specimens to be examined and pronounced upon. As the work on his books progressed, Ray would make a bundle of the finished manuscript, and this too the carrier was charged to deliver.

Ray's greatest work was the preparation of his *History of Plants* (1686) in which he described and classified more than eleven thousand species, most of which he had personally seen and examined. It was an enormous task, and of itself would have been considered sufficient justification for any one man's life's work. For two hundred years and more it was the standard classic on the subject. And all John Ray received for it was £5. No wonder he remained a poor man. He seems to have had no gift at all for managing his money affairs, and no doubt his publishers were quick to make use of their advantage over him.

The importance of his *History of Plants* lay not only in the fact that it contained descriptions of all known plants, but that, in a general introduction, it outlined the science of botany as Ray had slowly evolved it from the confusion of earlier writers.

Classification was Ray's first concern; but his interest in plants compelled him to study other aspects of plant life. He carried out experiments in the movement of sap in trees. He was one of the first to understand the sexual life of plants. He noted that the age of trees could be told by the 'rings' inside the bark, one for every year. But it is impossible even to begin to list the discoveries he made – discoveries which we now take for granted but which were often startling enough to be doubted at the time. In fact, no man hitherto had known so much as Ray knew about plants and plant-life in general.

But with this important book his work was by no means done. It was never done. No sooner had he written *Finis* to one book than he was busy planning another. After plants, he turned his attention to birds; then to fishes; then to insects – and he was studying these when he died.

Nor was this all. He had always been a deeply religious man. And so, in addition to his many books on the various aspects of natural history, he wrote, from time to time, religious books. Of these perhaps *The Wisdom of God* was the most important. Its full title explains the book's intention: *The Wisdom of God manifested in the Works of Creation.* It was published in 1691.

Properly to appreciate this book, which grew from a slim volume of 249 pages in its first edition to one of 464 pages in its third, it is necessary to remember that it was written two and a half centuries ago and that there was then no questioning the belief that all nature, from the smallest insect to the biggest mammal, from the pebble on the sea-shore to the stars in their courses, was but the manifestation of the Mind of God.

Today we would find Ray's attitude, as expressed in his books, too simple, even at times naive; but in his own day, and for a long while afterwards, it was entirely acceptable. The processes of nature were considered essentially religious. 'How manifest are all Thy works, O Lord,' Ray could say with the Psalmist, 'in wisdom Thou hast made them all.'

Yet at the same time (and this is its significance) *The Wisdom of God* is a scientific book. Whereas all Ray's books, so far, had been concerned with the task of identify-ing, describing and classifying, in this latest book he is concerned with interpreting. There is, he says, nothing accidental in nature, nothing arbitrary: all is according to plan – and the scientist's duty is to discover what that plan is. Ray examines countless examples of the working of nature, from the migration of birds to the behaviour of bees, and finds nothing that contradicts his conviction that all is according to 'the wisdom of God.'

Some reproach methinks it is to learned men (he says), that there should be so many animals still in the world whose outward shape is not yet taken notice of or described, much less their way of generation, food, manners, uses, observed. If man ought to reflect upon his Creator the glory of all his works, then ought he to take notice of them all and not to think anything unworthy of his cognizance.

It may be, he suggests, 'part of our business and employment in eternity to contemplate the Works of God ... I am sure it is part of the business of a Sabbath Day.'

In estimating Ray the botanist we should remember this book no less than his purely scientific ones, not only because it 'places' him in his period but also because it gives us a key to the appreciation of his character. He was as scientific in his examination of life as he was religious in his acceptance of it; and perhaps it was just this that made him, in spite of all his handicaps, the continually contented man he was.

Moreover, the older he grew, the more severe his handicaps became. To poverty was now added increasingly serious illness. But the work went on. Almost bed-ridden at last, he depended more and more upon others; and from various scraps and hints among his writings we may construct a picture of his wife and four little children all lending a hand.

For instance: of a certain moth (Dr Raven thinks it was the Burnished Brass) Ray writes, 'at the beginning of summer my little daughters caught many of this species flying at dusk in our garden.' Jane, the youngest, was finding caterpillars and catching moths for her father when she was only four years old. His wife, too, made her contribution. One night, for example, she chanced to go into a room where a female moth had just emerged from the chrysalis which Ray had shut up in a cage. The window was open and two male moths, she noticed, had entered and were flying round the room, from which Ray drew the conclusion that they were attracted in by the scent of the female – the first recording of a fact since commonly established. Nor was it only his family who helped. The villagers, too, were called upon and proudly brought their finds to Dewlands.

In July, 1695, for instance, the villagers brought him, within a few days, a Purple Emperor and a White Admiral, the first specimens ever to be described. Beetles, glow-worms, caterpillars, all sorts of creatures thus found their way into the invalid's hands; and if sometimes, the simple givers laughed at the old man's serious interest in these things, as villagers do, certainly they also loved and respected him and were grieved to see how surely the end was now near.

Sometimes, in fact, Ray felt he must give in at last. 'My glass,' he wrote, 'is almost out, and I am so afflicted with pains, that I have no heart to proceed any further.' But the despair, if not the pains, would pass, and back he would go to his work.

But the fire, once so unquenchable, was petering out. On January 7th, 1705, he wrote a letter to his friend and helper, Sir Hans Sloane, the founder of the British Museum.

'Dear Sir, the best of friends,' it read, 'These are to take a final leave of you as of this world. I look upon myself as a dying man. God requite your kindness expressed always towards me an hundredfold, bless you with a confluence of all good things in this world and eternal life and happiness hereafter, and grant us a happy meeting in heaven.'

Ten days later, in his seventy-eighth year, he died.

One would never guess, from all the thousands of words he wrote, the turbulence of the times through which Ray lived: he makes no mention of any of the troubles that beset his country: his concern was solely with his work. Yet it would be a mistake to suppose he was therefore a dull man.

A dull man does not make a multitude of friends, as Ray did. Nor would a dull man have thanked God, as he did, that he was privileged to live in an age of great change, when everything was struggling towards a new order. Most would have found it a hindrance: to Ray it was a help – the spur, in fact, that urged him on in the work he set himself to do.

The pity is that nobody should have thought to give posterity a full and close-up portrait of this 'most celebrated and worthy author.' One early biographer, William Derham, did write this of him: 'In his dealings, no man more strictly just; in his conversation, no man more humble, courteous and affable; towards God, no man more devout; and towards the poor and distressed, no man more compassionate and charitable, according to his abilities.' For the rest, we can only discover him in his books and that is hard to do. It has taken the patient industry and sympathy of Dr Raven to piece together some sort of a portrait from a word here, a hint there, and for this labour of love and scholarship we should be grateful. For we know something at least now of how extraordinary this 'very extraordinary man' was. All the great natural historians who followed him owed him an incalculable debt, since he it was who cleared away the ignorance and superstition and confusion that had beset this study hitherto. And every time any of us take pleasure in the study of nature in all her variety we are unwittingly saying our thanks to the village blacksmith's son, 'the excellent Mr Ray.'

Dick Turpin

THE STRANGE thing about Dick Turpin is that, gangster, thief and murderer though he was, he nevertheless became a national hero. It is now more than two hundred years since he was hanged, but he still remains one of the best-known and fondly regarded figures in the English story – and not only in Essex, where he was born and where many of his adventures took place, but all over the country and even abroad.

People who would respond with a blank look and a dumb answer if asked who William Caxton was, or many another British benefactor of mankind, know very well who Dick Turpin was, even if they are perhaps a little hazy about the facts. Crime, we are warned, does not pay; and certainly in the end it brought even Dick Turpin to the gallows; but it also brought him, both in his lifetime and posthumously, a measure of fame and popularity that only now shows signs of diminishing.

So many legends grew up around the life and exploits of this famous highwayman that it is not easy to sort out truth from fiction. Just as there are churches all over the country where Cromwell is supposed to have stabled his horses during the Civil War, and mansions by the score where Queen Elizabeth is supposed to have slept on one or other of her numerous progresses through the land, so there are countless inns which claim association with Dick Turpin, innumerable oak trees wherein he hid from his pursuers, and moats over which he leapt on his famous horse, Black Bess. Sometimes, no doubt, there is a certain amount of justification for these claims, but sometimes, also, they are nothing more than catch-penny tricks to lure the tourist.

And there is another hindrance to the discovery of the truth about Dick Turpin. One of the commonest ways of spreading news and perpetuating events two hundred years ago was by means of the broadsheet and chapbook – hand-printed news-sheets and pamphlets (often in rhyme) that were hawked in the street, or sold from door to door. Their aim was less to tell the truth than to provide a cheap and lively memento of the latest popular sensation, though of course they often passed for truth among the ignorant masses at a time when there was little opportunity (and perhaps little inclination) to check the facts. By the dozen these broadsheets, whose jingle was intended to increase their popularity and to enable the buyer to commit them to memory, told of Dick Turpin's exploits, until gradually there was built up a picture that fixed itself in the common mind and passed for truth.

But at last we know, more or less, the real story of this so-called Knight of the Open Road. It was left to two Americans, Arty Ash and Julius Day, to search all possible sources for the real facts of the case, until, from newspapers, records, and documents unearthed here, there and everywhere, they were able to tell the story much as it actually happened, and not as it was supposed to have happened.

The Americans' task was not an easy one, but they set about it with a thoroughness which American students often employ when exploring the by-roads of English history. They called their book *Immortal Turpin* (it was published in

1948) and any account of Dick Turpin today or in the future must necessarily be considerably indebted to it.

Admittedly, the portrait that now emerges is a great deal less flattering than the one which has so long persisted in popular fancy. If anything, it even deepens the mystery why so lawless and dangerous a character should have won such a widespread regard. All the same, it remains an intriguing picture. Dick Turpin may have been a gangster, but he was somehow a gangster with a difference. And if, as now appears likely, some of his best-known exploits – such as, for instance, the famous ride to York – never took place at all, those that did take place are often of sufficient daring to capture our imagination across the centuries.

Dick Turpin was born on Sept 21, 1705, in the village of Hempstead, not far from Thaxted, in the NW corner of Essex. His father seems to have followed the double calling of butcher and inn-keeper, which is hardly surprising, since Hempstead, small as it is today, was even smaller then, and neither trade would of itself have constituted a full-time job.

The inn was the *Bell*; and, although today it has changed its name to *Rose and Crown*, it still stands at the quiet crossroads, a substantial timber-and-plaster building that probably looks much the same now as it did when Dick ran about its low-ceilinged rooms as a little boy.

What sort of a life he led in those early years we can only guess: the one fact we know about them is that he attended the village school, being taught to read and write by a schoolmaster named Smith who, years later, when his one-time pupil had become notorious throughout the land, was to be the chief cause of bringing him to justice.

It may have been during these boyhood years that Dick caught the smallpox which so badly scarred his face that when, finally, a public proclamation offered a substantial reward for his apprehension, he was described as having 'a brown complexion very much marked with the small pox.' Almost certainly, too, he was a typically healthy and well-set up country lad, for this same official proclamation (though he was then thirty years old) declared him to be about five feet nine inches tall, 'pretty upright and broad about the shoulders.'

At sixteen it was decided that he should follow his father's second calling, and he was apprenticed for five years to a butcher in Whitechapel. Thus he made his early acquaintance with the East End of London, whose dark alleys and disreputable inns – eighteenth-century London at its worst – were so often in the future to provide him with convenient hiding-places. Apprentices in those days, as we know, were apt to be badly treated, their masters being more concerned to add the fees of apprenticeship to their incomes than to teach the apprentices their future trade; and it was nothing uncommon for the starved and ill-treated boys to run away, even if they dared not go home. Young Dick Turpin, however, stayed the full five years, and so perhaps we may assume that he was as fortunate in his master as he was skilful at his work. Anyhow, the next we hear of him is sometime after 1728 when he set up as a butcher in his own right at Thaxted, the town he must already have known very well. In that year, too, he had married Betty Millington, who was a servant at the Hempstead home of Mr Smith's father, the village schoolmaster.

And so, at twenty-three, Dick Turpin was already a married man with a little business of his own and a promising future. What, then, could it have been that caused him – and in so short a time – to throw away his prospects and embark upon a life of crime? It is a question to which, even now, we can give no satisfactory answer. Might there have been, perhaps, some unsatisfactory strain in his character that only waited for a favourable opportunity to come uppermost and finally to take charge altogether?

However it may have been, he quitted Thaxted after a surprisingly short stay and changed his address first to Enfield and then to Sewardstone, in Essex.

But he was no more successful as a butcher in Sewardstone than he had been in Thaxted. He soon got into debt. And that, maybe, was the cause of all the trouble. It seems that, unable to pay his meat bills, he decided to try his hand at cattle stealing. He must have been desperate to have embarked upon such a course, for cattle stealing, in the eighteenth century, was a hanging offence, and there was little likelihood that he would get away with it for long.

But it was always to be one of the most remarkable things about Dick Turpin that, however near he came, time and time again, to being captured, he somehow always seemed to manage to escape just in time. And so it was at Sewardstone. The thefts were proved; the constable arrived to arrest him; but the thief, forewarned, had vanished.

His first hiding-place was in the Rodings, those lonely, arable, sparsely populated villages where even today a man may go for miles and never meet a soul. From there he made his way to Canvey Island, off the Essex coast; and here he fell in with a band of smugglers, who had their headquarters in the ruins of Hadleigh Castle, close in shore.

Essex, with its maze of estuaries, whose tortuous channels provided a ready means of avoiding detection for those who knew their way about them, has always been famous for its smugglers. All manner of contraband, from spirits to silks, was run across from the Continent under cover of darkness and then unloaded into small craft that were skilfully piloted through the reedy channels to selected hiding-places. Hadleigh Castle, a mere shell of a building today, was an obvious choice for the smugglers; but this particular gang (or so the story runs) took the extra precaution of burning coloured lights in the ruins at night, so that the local country folk, supposing the place to be haunted, gave it a wide berth.

But smuggling of this kind is essentially a job for men who are used to the sea, and Turpin was a landsman born and bred: not surprisingly, therefore, he did not stay long with his new friends. Nevertheless, brief as this episode in his story is, it is important; for it gave him his first taste of the life of the outlaw and thereby helped to shape his future course. Given luck and cunning, fearlessness and a strong right arm, it seemed that a man could find more profitable (and easier) ways of making money than by working for it.

Leaving the gang of smugglers, Turpin made his way inland to the familiar cover of Epping Forest. Here he turned first deer-stealer and then house-breaker. The Forest was a favourite haunt of thieves, since it provided them with ample cover. What the winding, twining channels of the Essex estuaries were to the smuggler, the deep groves and bushy tracks of the Essex forest were to the thief and robber.

One band of thieves in particular had its hiding-place here: it was known as Gregory's Gang; and soon Turpin had joined their company. Their plan was to raid the larger houses in the neighbourhood of the Forest and then flee back to cover with their spoils. There was plenty of loot to be had for those who knew the way to get it. Banks were not the common use of everybody, as they are today: many a farmer and landed gentleman kept the best part of his wealth at home in secret cupboards, hiding-places about the house, and even in locked chests.

Turpin was soon initiated into the tricks of the thief's trade, and took his share of danger with the rest. He had discovered a way of life that clearly suited him; and soon there was neither the opportunity nor the desire to turn back. In fact, he had joined the ranks of that great army of outlaws who roamed the English countryside in the eighteenth century, doing very much as they pleased.

Gregory's Gang became in time so strong a menace to the population that a price was put on their heads. A reward of fifty pounds apiece was offered to whoever should give evidence leading to their arrest. It is worth quoting from the proclamation which announced this reward because it throws a considerable light on the gang's methods:

Whitehall, February 11*th*, 1735

Whereas it has been represented to His Majesty that on Tuesday, the Fourth Day of February instant, Five Horsemen armed each with a Case of Pistols, came about seven o'clock in the evening to the house of Joseph Lawrence the Elder, being part of a Farm called Earlesbury Farm, near Edgeware in the County of Middlesex, and went into the Sheep-house, where a Servant was, whose hands they tied behind him, and by threatening to shoot him, and clapping Pistols to his Body, compelled him to go with them to his Master's, the said Joseph Lawrence's House in order to get the Door opened which was accordingly done and they all then entered the house with Pistols in their Hands, in which was the said Joseph Lawrence, who is an Ancient Man of upwards of Seventy years of Age, a Servant Man and Maid, that they bound the said Man and Maid and forced the Master upstairs to show them where his Money was and broke open all the Doors, Chests and Places and thoroughly searched every part of the House and not finding the Money they expected, upon their coming down stairs most inhumanly and barbarously abused the said Joseph Lawrence by beating him with a stick till they broke it to pieces, letting down his Breeches and Whipping him in a Violent manner, that they likewise laid a faggot on the Fire and laid him down by it and threatened to burn him, then took a Knife and Drew it under his Throat and afterwards dragged him by the Hair of his Head about the Kitchen, then took a Kettle of Water off the Fire and threw the water upon him. That they took from the house of the said Joseph, about Twenty Five Pounds in Money, one Silver Cup, several Silver Spoons and all the Linnen in the House ... and so on.

A reward of fifty pounds was worth far more in 1735 than it is worth today, and so it is not surprising that four days after the Proclamation was published and prominently posted about the countryside, three of Gregory's Gang were arrested. Soon after, Gregory himself, the ring-leader, was also caught.

Turpin, who had fled into hiding somewhere in London, must have realised that the game was up, at least as far as house-breaking with this particular gang was concerned; and it was now that he decided to turn highwayman and so embarked upon that swift and daring series of adventures that were destined to bring him so strange a fame and so sorry an end.

He knew well enough the risks he was taking. His name was already familiar to the public by reason of his part in the Gregory Gang's activities. But in any case there was no alternative: he had started on a journey from which there was no return. House-breakers worked best in parties; but the highwayman fared best alone – or at most with one other person. The newspapers of that summer and autumn (1735) contained accounts of highway robberies which showed that 'Turpin the Butcher' had lined up with 'Rowden the Pewterer'; and together they were holding up citizens on the outskirts of London.

Turpin soon showed that he was no ordinary highwayman, as witness this newspaper account of a robbery that took place on Putney Heath late that autumn.

> Tuesday at four in the Afternoon, Mr Tebb a Grocer, opposite the George Inn, in Little Drury Lane, was robb'd by two Highwaymen just by the Gibbet on Putney Heath, they made him dismount and searched all his pockets, and took from him £7 5s and then made off. One of them had the impudence to tell him he was Turpin, and bid him remember how civilly he had used him.

The partnership with Rowden does not seem to have lasted long, for, by the spring of 1736, Turpin was joined by one of the most famous highwaymen of the day, Bob King, known as the Gentleman Highwayman for his distinctive dress and persuasive manners. Birds of a feather flock together; and it was typical of Turpin, who was himself far removed from the usual eighteenth-century cut-throat ruffian, that he should join forces with this spectacular Bob King.

It is not easy for us, in these days of smooth roads and speedy traffic, to realise with anything like exactitude the state of the English highway in the eighteenth century. Early writers, such as Smollett and Fielding and Defoe, have left us plenty of descriptions of the conditions then prevailing, but they picture a countryside so different from ours that we have difficulty in bridging the gap.

To begin with, each parish had to maintain the roads within its boundaries, and this was done by compelling farmers to give six days a year of unpaid labour for their upkeep. Since the farmers were neither interested nor skilled in the job, and there was no supervisor, it can be imagined how ineffectively the work was done. In fact, the state of the roads, even the best of them, was such that wheeled traffic was quite impossible on them in winter, and the only satisfactory mode of travel was on horseback: even this was made difficult by the teams of pack-horses that blocked the way.

Then again there were stretches of wild land – scrub and bush – all over England, and these provided the best possible hiding-places for footpads and robbers of every kind. The traveller took to the road at the peril of losing not only his purse but his life. In addition to the vast stretches of heath-land, there were the forests; and the roads through these were specially dangerous.

It was inevitable that Turpin should choose such places for the pursuit of his lawless calling, and where more likely than Epping Forest, so well-known to him from his earliest days? It was here, therefore, that the majority of his exploits in future were to take place and soon his infamous deeds became the talk of Essex.

Deep in the Forest there was a cave which Turpin had used in his deer-stealing days. This now became his head-quarters. From here he would sally forth on his horse to rob any wealthy traveller who was unlucky enough to come his way; and here he would return with his booty, to rest and hide until he felt it was safe to venture out on the next exploit. No doubt his proven friends visited the cave. It was even said that his wife supplied him with food and clothes, and frequently remained in the hideout with him.

Nobody in the neighbourhood felt safe. Travellers who went by coach took to carrying guns, and even pedlars and higglers armed themselves against possible attack. Turpin knew, of course, that he was being sought for, and one of the precautions he took (as also did King, his confederate) was to have his horse shod with circular shoes, so that his pursuers should not be able to tell, from the horses' imprints, whether he was coming or going.

Early in May, 1737, Turpin had the misfortune to shoot his friend King by accident. It happened this way. Turpin and King had stopped a man in the Forest and robbed him, after which King exchanged horses with him, taking the new mount to an inn in Whitechapel, where he said he would collect it next day. By a fortunate coincidence the robbed man also went to the inn and saw his horse being watered by the ostler.

'... And about four o'clock (so the report contin-ues) Matthew King came for the mare and being stopped confessed that his brother Robert King was in Gloucester Street in Goodman's Fields on Foot, with

Turpin on Horseback, where being taken Turpin fired, shot King in the left Breast and rode off. The two Brothers were carried before Justice Ricketts, Robert was committed to the New Prison and Matthew to Bridewell. There were found upon Robert King a brace of Pistols and a bag of bullets.'

The loss of his friend was a hard blow for Turpin. From now on he worked alone, a man with a heavy price on his head, a man who ran severe risks at every turn. But risks had never yet deterred him: very likely he even thrived on them, dare-devil that he was; and we soon hear of him back at the old game.

Not everybody, however, looked on Turpin as a hero. He had plenty of enemies as well, and now the chase was pursued in earnest, particularly by the Keepers of the Forest. But Turpin knew the Forest as well as they did, perhaps even better. Admittedly, one of them succeeded in tracking him down, but all he got for his trouble was to be shot dead on the spot. It was on this occasion, incidentally, that Turpin clambered up an oak tree to avoid his followers and hid there (or so the story goes) for two days and a night without being discovered. This sounds like a tall story, more fiction than fact; but there is no doubt that Turpin often performed the incredible, and some at least of the tall stories connected with his name had a foundation in fact. At any rate, one way or another he continued to evade his enemies without in the slightest diminishing his activities as the 'Terror of the Essex Roads.' He was like a will-o'-the-wisp. There was no catching him – though newspapers sometimes reported his capture and on one occasion were so anxious to inform their readers of the fact that three of them, on the same day, described how he was now safely bestowed in three different prisons.

It was not his fearlessness alone that caused him to be so attractive a figure in the eyes of a large part of the populace – that part, almost certainly, which, being themselves neither rich nor travellers, had nothing to fear from him. There was at least a hint of Robin Hood in him; and if he never went so far as to rob the rich in order to give to the poor, as Robin boasted, at least it could he said that his robberies were only accompanied by violence when his victims showed fight.

A note in the *London Gazette* for June 7th, 1737, tells how:

> Yesterday in the afternoon about three o'clock as the Saffron Walden and Bishop's Stortford Stage-coaches were coming to Town, they were stopp'd about a Mile and a Half this side of Epping, by Turpin the Famous Highwayman, who took from the Walden Coach about Four Pounds. He used the Passengers with a great deal of Civility, and although there were above Twenty persons in and about both Coaches, and a Chaise in sight, he made off through the Wood without being taken.

But if his behaviour brought only admiration from one section of the community, another section was showing an increased impatience with the authorities for letting him so frequently (and, as they considered, easily) slip out of their clutches. Perhaps Turpin himself guessed that the noose round him would soon be drawn tighter and that he would find himself trapped at last. This, anyway, would seem to be the interpretation of his action on June 25th of this year.

On this day, in Epping Forest, he waylaid Sir Charles Turner, an influential gentleman from Lynn, in Norfolk; and, instead of robbing him, he merely asked a favour. 'Sir Charles Turner,' he said, 'I am Turpin, and do not design to offer you any incivility or rob you of anything. In a little time I shall come to the gallows and hope that when I have occasion you will do me your best service.' It was a cunning gesture, but it served him to no purpose. When the time came, as it soon did, Sir Charles put forward no plea on Turpin's behalf: it would have been useless anyway.

Later in the month a notice appeared, daily, in every newspaper, announcing the fact that a reward of £200 was offered to anybody who should directly cause Turpin's arrest. Such a handsome amount was bound to attract informers. There were now eyes, Turpin must have felt, in every bush in the Forest; and it is not surprising that he decided to quit his old haunts and ply his risky trade where there was perhaps less chance of his being discovered. And so, eventually, he came to Yorkshire, where the wide, unpeopled moors promised as effective a screen for his robberies as that which he had so long enjoyed in Epping Forest.

He made York itself, with its narrow, winding back streets, his headquarters, and gave himself the new name of John Palmer. As John Palmer he was soon established as a respectable citizen and a sportsman. Indeed, he might well have succeeded in evading detection much longer than he did, if he had not one day committed a foolish prank (it was scarcely more) that proved his undoing.

As Turpin he had always been fond of the odd gesture, the boastful word, and so far he had always got away with it. But the pitcher can go to the well once too often. John

Palmer's foolish action, this time, was trifling enough; but the tales of crime and detection are full of instances where just such minor affairs serve to bring the criminal to book. Turpin (we will call him by his right name) had been out shooting with some friends. Arriving back at the inn where he was staying, he chanced to see one of the landlord's fowls straying in the street, shot at it, and killed it. A neighbour remonstrated with him. 'You should not,' he said, 'have shot your landlord's cockerel – it was wrong to do so.' Whereupon Turpin, with his old careless boastfulness, replied: 'If you wait a minute, while I change my piece, I'll shoot you too.' The neighbour of course, was annoyed and informed the owner of the bird of what had happened, who proceeded to lodge a complaint with the constable. From this trifling incident all the rest followed in quick succession.

Turpin was arrested. The magistrate, suspicious of his story, made enquiries. Even now, under the name of John Palmer, Turpin might have avoided detection had it not been for an unlucky coincidence. From behind prison bars, at York Castle, where he awaited trial, he wrote to his brother-in-law, in Hempstead, asking for a character that would prevent him from being apprehended, but the letter never reached its intended recipient. It was, for some reason, returned to the post office in Hempstead, where, by the oddest chance, it was seen by Mr Smith, Turpin's one-time schoolmaster. Smith recognised the handwriting, and, no doubt having in mind the reward of £200, informed the police. The letter was opened, the identity of John Palmer was revealed. Just to make doubly sure, Smith was sent to York to identify his former pupil. Turpin's fate was now sealed.

The strange thing is that, even now he does not seem to have thought he would hang for his offences as highwayman – whatever they might do to him for shooting his landlord's cockerel. His arrogant faith in himself never forsook him.

Admittedly, Turpin had some sort of reason to support his conviction that he would yet go free. Most of his confederates of former days were dead: they could not inform against him. And he learned now, if he did not know already, just how strongly the mass of public opinion appeared to be on his side. The prisoner, in those days, though he might be bound in chains and kept behind bars, was allowed to see his friends and to receive whatever gifts they cared to bring. Turpin, in York Castle, was visited by crowds of people; he was regaled with food and drink; he was made to feel more like a hero than a doomed criminal. No wonder he failed to realise how slender now his chances really were.

It was on March 22, 1739, that Turpin's trial took place. For nine years he had evaded capture, roaming the countryside at will and establishing himself as the most daring and successful highwayman of his day; but at last the game was up. A full and verbatim account of the trial exists in the York Castle records. Various witnesses were called, the prisoner was questioned, and most cleverly the counsel succeeded in bringing the incriminating evidence to light. It must soon have been clear even to Turpin what the end would be, and presently he heard the Judge say: 'As your country has found you guilty of a crime worthy of death, it is my office to pronounce sentence against you.'

Turpin was removed to the condemned cell, called 'Pompey's Parlour,' and there he awaited his death. He remained arrogant and boastful, telling his friends of his adventures and drinking at their expense. An extract from the Press of the time gives some idea of the conditions he enjoyed.

> ... The whole country have flocked here to see him and have been very liberal to him in so much that he has wine constantly before him till his trial and 'tis said the Jailor has made £100 by selling liquor to him and his visitors. Though the fellow has made a great noise in the world he'll die like a dog.

He died, in fact, as he had lived, game to the end. The highwayman whose fine attire had always captured the people's fancy, ordered himself a new coat and shoes for the hanging and hired five poor men to follow him to the gallows in mourning hats and gloves.

The place where Turpin was hanged is now, ironically enough, part of the York race-course known as Knavesmire. On the morning of Saturday, April 7th, 1739, Turpin's chains were struck from him; he dressed himself in his new clothes; and, followed by his hired mourners, he mounted the cart and was driven through the huge crowds that had assembled to see the end. Rumour decorated that sorry end with various tales appropriate, as was supposed, to the occasion. It was said that Turpin bowed repeatedly to the crowds as the cart passed through them; that he showed extraordinary calm and indifference; that he presented the hangman with a small ivory whistle; and that instead of letting himself he slowly hanged as the rope took his weight, he flung himself from the ladder and so died instantaneously. Be all this as it may, the plain, certain fact is that in York that day Turpin met the fate he had been seeking through nine adventurous but disreputable years.

The event was a nation-wide sensation. Turpin the man was dead, long live Turpin the legend! From printing-presses all over the land there poured a spate of broadsheets and ballads and chapbooks extolling the story of 'bold Turpin that mischievous Blade.' His name became a household word; he was admired by some for his saucy daring and reviled by others for his thieving and bloodshed.

A hundred years was not long enough to dispel the legend he had become. And then, in 1834, it was given a new and even more vigorous lease of life. Harrison Ainsworth, the popular novelist, made him the hero of a novel, *Rookwood*, that immediately caught the popular fancy. As novelists sometimes will, Ainsworth distorted the facts to suit his own ends, but his chief contribution was to create Black Bess, the mare that served her master so well and brought him safely out of so many dangers. Black Bess, perhaps, was Ainsworth's master-stroke; for the English simply cannot resist the story of a fleet and trusty horse. And so to the legend of Turpin was added the legend of Black Bess, a combination that could not fail. After the appearance of *Rookwood*, fact and fiction soon became so inextricably mixed in the popular mind that nobody knew – or even cared – which was which.

For another hundred years the Turpin story survived, but now it begins to look as if at last the end were in sight. An age of enquiry has dawned: we are all interested today in facts. Many a popular fancy is wilting under our sceptical gaze; and Turpin is no exception. All the same, two hundred years is a long while for a sham fame to last. Turpin certainly has had a long run for his money.

John Constable

BROADLY SPEAKING, artists may he divided into two kinds: those who paint more or less in the same manner as their predecessors, and those who paint like nobody but themselves. There are, in fact, the conventional artists and the innovators. And, naturally, it is the conventional artists who are more likely to achieve popularity in their own time, whilst the innovators will probably have to wait until they are dead to be accorded the recognition they deserve.

The reason for this is clear. We, the general public, prefer an artist to paint things as *we* see them (only, so to speak, more so) and not as *he* sees them. We like to feel 'at home' when we look at pictures; comfortably excited; deliciously reminded of the scenes we ourselves have enjoyed, exclaiming 'Look! isn't that lovely!' If the artist sees things quite differently from the way we see them, and insists on trying to express that difference in his pictures, then we are baffled. He makes us feel uncomfortable and not at all 'at home.' So we either tend (at best) to dismiss him as uninteresting, or (at worst) to scorn him as a sham.

Yet by such an attitude we may very well be proclaiming our own unwillingness to get out of the comfortable groove of what-we-are-used-to. Which is not at all to say that every artist who paints in the conventional manner is a bad artist, or that every artist who strikes out into new paths, painting like nobody but himself, is a good artist.

But let a painter express all this in his own words. They

need our concentrated attention if we are to get their full meaning, but the effort is well worth while. Here is what he says:

In art, there áre two modes by which men aim at distinction. In the one, by a careful application to what others have accomplished, the artist imitates their works, or selects and combines their various beauties; in the other, he seeks excellence at its primitive source, nature. In the first, he forms a style upon the study of pictures, and produces either imitative or eclectic art; in the second, by a close observation of nature, he discovers qualities existing in her which have never been portrayed before, and thus forms a style which is original. The results of the one mode, as they repeat that with which the eye is already familiar, are soon recognised and estimated, while the advances of the artist in a new path must necessarily be slow, for few are able to judge of that which deviates from the usual course, or are qualified to appreciate original studies.

The writer of these words was John Constable, England's greatest landscape painter; and they exactly illustrate his own case. As an artist he was an innovator, striking out in a new path, and, as such, he was slow to win the fame his art deserved.

Many thousands of pounds are eagerly paid today for his canvases; but in his lifetime he had difficulty in selling them at all. He painted portraits at fifteen guineas a head, and the most he ever received, even for the largest of his pictures, was about a hundred pounds.

We can all enjoy Constable's pictures now. Indeed, he is one of the most admired of all British artists. But in his own time there were very few who recognised his genius. However, he knew his own worth. In words that remind us of the doomed and youthful Keats ('I know I shall be among the immortals') Constable said, when he was at the very beginning of his career, 'I feel now, more than ever, a decided conviction that I shall sometime or other make some good pictures – pictures that shall be valuable to posterity, if I reap not the benefit of them.' This conviction continued to support him, in the face of poverty and lack of proper recognition, and the few who did praise him with understanding were his sufficient comfort. 'I have my admirers,' he said, 'each one of whom I consider an host.'

John Constable was born on June 11th, 1776, at East Bergholt, on the river Stour which forms the boundary between Essex and Suffolk. His father was a fairly well-to-do miller, the owner of three or four mills in the neighbourhood. When he was seven, John was sent to a boarding-school at Lavenham, not far away; but the headmaster seems to have left the care of his pupils mainly to the usher, who flogged them so unmercifully that everybody hated him; and John was accordingly removed to Dedham (Essex) Grammar School. Here, under the wise and sympathetic Dr Grimwood, he fared much better. He was never much of a scholar, however, his best subject being, we are told, penmanship. The truth is that John's thoughts were not on his books: he was already interested in one thing above all others, namely painting.

It was his preoccupation with art that attracted him in close friendship to John Dunthorne, a plumber and glazier who lived in a little cottage close to the gates of his father's house. Windows, in those days, were glazed in a framework of lead, instead of, as now, wood; and the village glazier used to set out in the morning, with a bag over his back and sheets of glass, to tramp the neighbourhood and mend windows wherever he was asked to do so. Often he covered many miles a day. He was one of those itinerant tradesmen, like the knife-grinder and the chair-mender, who have now almost disappeared from rural life. John Dunthorne was, in fact, a countryman to the core – and a remarkable one at that. He spent all the time he could spare from his work in painting the country scenes which he knew and loved so well. It was their common delight in art that drew these two lads together in a bond which remained fast until Dunthorne's death, and, indeed, was renewed with his son.

Constable's father intended him for the Church, but he showed no inclination for the necessary studies, and so it was decided that he should follow in his father's footsteps and become a miller. For the best part of a year, therefore, he worked in one of his father's mills.

This fact is important. Wind and weather are the miller's concern, and Constable was early trained to observe these things with a strict and knowledgeable eye. Nobody, in the years to come, was to paint clouds as well as he did, and the weather was indicated in all his pictures to such a pitch of realism that Fuseli, a fashionable painter of the time, said, on seeing one of Constable's paintings of showers, that it made him 'call for his great coat and umbrella.'

And it was not only his ability to get the weather into his pictures that Constable the painter owed to Constable the miller: he sought, all his life, to fill his canvases with the close, informed love of nature which he had enjoyed in those early years. It was the banks of the river Stour, he said and especially the rich valley of Dedham, that made him a painter.

> The sound of water escaping from mill-dams, etc., willows, old rotten planks, slimy posts, and brickwork, I love such things. Shakespeare could make everything poetical; he tells us of poor Tom's haunts among 'sheep cotes and mills.' As long as I do paint, I shall never cease to paint such places.

And in fact the last picture Constable ever painted, the one he was engaged upon when he died, was of a mill.

It was in this exact, pulsing reproduction of the rural scene, especially the lower reaches of the river Stour, that Constable differed from all landscape painters who had preceded him. The fashion was all for a classical, stylised representation of nature – a refinement of the actual scene inhabited by piping shepherd boys and be-ribboned shepherdesses, where rain never wetted anybody nor mud dirtied the dainty shoes, and rough work in winter fields was something the polite person never mentioned. Against this genteel view of the rural scene Constable was in deep and continual revolt. Painting, he used to say, was only another word with him for feeling, and his feeling for nature was the genuine countryman's. In this revolt against the classical he was, of course, in key with the poets of his day, Wordsworth and the other members of the so-called Romantic Revival. The emphasis in art was shifting from the urban to the rural, from the polite to the real.

Even Constable's colours were new and startling to eyes used to the dim browns and dark hues of the classical painters. There is a story which well illustrates this. One of the

patrons and great amateurs of art at that time was Sir
George Beaumont, of Cole Orton Hall, whose collection of
Old Masters was famous and who himself was something of
an artist. Constable was invited to go and stay awhile at Cole
Orton; and one day, while Sir George was extolling the
subdued tones of the Old Masters (no doubt, though tact-
fully, hinting that Constable's own colours were far too
bold) he fetched a Cremona violin and said in effect that
this should be the prevailing tone that painters ought to aim
at. For answer, Constable took the violin and laid it on the
lawn in front of the house against the throbbing, life-filled
green of the grass.

On another occasion, Sir George, loving, as he did, the
autumnal browns and believing they should find a place
somewhere in any landscape, asked Constable, 'Do you not
find it difficult to determine where to place your *brown
tree*?' 'Not in the least,' Constable replied: 'I never put such
a thing in a picture.'

The country, so to speak, was in Constable's blood – the
deep, the real country. 'A gentleman's park,' he once said,
'is my aversion.' And his pictures are all expressions of this
aversion, being each a depiction of the countryside as it is
and not as a fastidious taste might wish it to be. His clouds
are the clouds a miller might watch, knowing what they
portended and aware of the currents that controlled them.
His countrymen are workers on the land – men and women
whose daily bread depends upon the fields and woods and
meadows which urban eyes consider as so much scenery. His
mills would grind corn, his cottages are no better or worse
than the hundreds of thatched and half-timbered farm-
cottages with which he was familiar at home, and his trees
(look, for instance, at the *Study of an Elm Tree*, with its

crusty bark on which one could break the skin of one's knuckles) are the living trees he had loved all his days – trees that climbed to the light, dripped rain in winter, gave shade in summer, fed on the earth with their burying, wide-spread roots and renewed it again with the compost of their dead leaves. Even his rainbows startle, as rainbows do, and veil the scene with their transparent spectrum where they touch the ground.

All this we find easy to appreciate in Constable today, whether it be in the famous *Haywain* in the National Gallery, with Flatford Mill itself (one of his father's mills) beside the cool stream; or in *The Cornfield*, also in the National Gallery, with its farm-boy lying on his belly to drink from the summer pool and Dedham church tower providing (as it so often did) a happy focus for the distant scene. So that it is difficult for us to realise how strange these pictures seemed to the general public of his day.

Constable's lot would have been made a great deal happier if he had been able to marry when he wanted to. He had, in his twenties, fallen in love with Maria Bicknell, whose grand-father, Dr Rhudde, was the wealthy rector of Bergholt, where, most probably, the two first met. Dr Rhudde, in fact, was the villain of the piece. It was he, rather than Maria's father, who objected to the marriage; and, since the doctor was so wealthy, Mr Bicknell seems to have deferred to his wishes in the matter, lest Maria should forfeit the fortune she might reasonably expect to inherit from him. At any rate, permission to marry was withheld, and Maria, out of love for and in deference to her parents, refused to marry without permission. Even letters between her and the impe-cunious young artist were forbidden, though to this extent at least Maria rebelled and corresponded in secret.

In spite of all, Constable never gave up hope. 'Be assured,' he wrote to Maria, 'we have only to consider our union as an event that must happen, and we shall yet be happy.' But it was not until 1816, when he was already forty years old, that the marriage finally took place; and Mr Bicknell, unable any longer to refrain from knowing Constable, found on acquaintance that he was even growing fond of him.

Dr Rhudde, however, was less easily won over; and when he died, three years after her marriage, Maria must indeed have been surprised to find that he had bequeathed to her a legacy of £4,000. About this time, Constable's own father died; and when the property was divided among the family, his share amounted to another £4,000.

It looked as if the hardest times, so far as their financial difficulties were concerned, were over. But Constable, like so many artists, who are too absorbed in their work to spend their energy in driving bargains, was never a good manager of his affairs. He was as likely to give away a picture to a friend as to sell it to a dealer. It had always been this way with him. His friend and biographer, C R Leslie, wrote of him in his earlier years that

> Although he was an early riser, frugal in his habits of living, and not addicted to any vicious extravagance either of time or money, yet neither was he an economist. Both were always too readily at the disposal of others; it was as difficult for him to say no to a borrower, as to shut his door against a lounger, still less could he ever resist an appeal to his charity; and if a book or a print he wanted came in his way, the chances were he would buy it, though with the money that should pay for his next day's dinner.

The habit, thus formed with him in his early manhood, when he was single, stayed with him when he became a husband and father. 'My finances are sadly deranged,' was a complaint intermittently to be heard from him almost to the end.

Only in the country was Constable really happy. In his twenties, when his parents had reconciled themselves to his determination to devote himself to art, he chafed continually at the necessity to spend so much time in London. 'I have hardly yet got reconciled to brick walls, and dirty streets, after leaving the endeared scenes of Suffolk.' And again: 'This fine weather almost makes me melancholy; it recalls so forcibly every scene we have visited and drawn together.'

The green Vale of Dedham was never out of his mind. 'I love every stile and stump, and every lane in the village, so deep rooted are early impressions.' With him those early impressions were the life-long foundations of all his art. 'You know,' he said to Maria, before she became his wife, 'I have always succeeded best with my native scenes.'

Not for him were either the mountains or the sea: they could not stir him like the level green meadowlands of home. Later he was to go to Brighton on several occasions, for the health of his wife and family; but he never really liked it. His description of it then is worth repeating. 'Ladies dressed and undressed; gentlemen in morning gowns and slippers, or without them or anything else, about knee-deep in the breakers; footmen, children, nursery-maids, boys, fishermen, and Preventive Service men with hangers and pistols; rotten fish, and those hideous, amphibious animals, the old bathing-women, whose language, both in oaths and voice, resembles men, all mixed together in endless and indecent confusion ... In short, there is nothing here for a painter but the breakers and the sky, which have been lovely indeed, and always varying.'

Similarly, on one occasion he made a tour, with a friend, of the Lake District, in search of subjects to draw and paint; and although he brought back with him a great number of sketches, they were more remarkable for their effects of light (a matter which interested him anywhere and everywhere) than for their general beauty. Such scenes of grandeur were not after his heart. Used to the wide, open skies and level meadows of the Stour, the mountains of Cumberland and Westmorland overawed him: their solitude oppressed one who was essentially sociable, a man fond of company.

Not that all the greatest of Constable's pictures were of his native region. Sometimes he could rise to equal heights in the depiction of quite different scenes. His closest and almost lifelong friend was John Fisher, who became the Archdeacon of Berkshire. It was while visiting him that he accumulated the many inspired sketches that ultimately flowered in the several great canvases of Salisbury Cathedral.

Constable's friendship for Fisher, in fact, was, next to his love for Maria, the most profound human influence of his life. He would report to Fisher the progress of his pictures, sure of a sympathetic understanding that was so signally lacking elsewhere. His pictures in the Academy might pass unnoticed or, worse, be scorned in favour of the flashy art that hung beside them on the walls; but in the Archdeacon he knew he had a deeply appreciative audience, and many of his finest works found their way into Fisher's home.

Encouragement, so rarely given, was nevertheless essential to Constable, as it is to all artists; but kindred spirits to such as he are rare indeed. In the end, only his own resolve, his own dedication to the art he had chosen, supported him.

When he was engaged on the large canvas of *The Cornfield*
he wrote to Fisher: 'My picture occupied me wholly: I could
think of and speak to no one. I felt like a relation of mine in
the Battle of Waterloo. He said he "dared not turn his head
right or left, but always kept it straight forward, thinking of
himself alone".'

Such concentration, exhausting like a fever, is the price
all great artists must pay, though the result, in their finished
pictures, may appear to us who enjoy them as calm as
sunlight on green fields. Discoverers, they stand 'silent on a
peak in Darien'; and in their pictures they give us the easy
enjoyment of the rapture they so hardly won.

Not that there was anything of the lonely god about
Constable: even fools he would suffer gladly. Leslie tells
many a tale in illustration of this, of which the following
must here suffice.

> Varley, the astrologer (Constable wrote in a letter
> to Leslie) has just called on me, and I have bought a
> little drawing of him. He told me how to '*do* land-
> scape,' and was so kind as to point out all my defects.
> The price of the drawing was 'a guinea and a half *to a
> gentleman*, and a guinea only *to an artist*,' but I
> insisted on his taking the larger sum as he had clearly
> proved to me that I was no artist.

On another occasion, Constable was invited to dinner to
meet a woman painter.

> 'I found,' he said, 'a laughing, ignorant, fat,
> uncouth old woman; but very good-natured; and she
> gave me no trouble, as she wanted no instruction from

me. When she told me of an oil proper for painting, I told her it would not do, and that she could give me no greater proof of it than that one of her pictures was painted entirely with it.'

It is a pity that Leslie is not able to tell us more exactly how gladly (or perhaps, in this case, not so gladly) Constable suffered yet another fool. All that Constable's letter says of this particular interview is: 'Mr Appleton, the tub-maker, of Tottenham Court Road, called to know if I had a damaged picture which I could let him have cheap, as he was fitting up a room.'

More revealing is this last instance of Constable's forbearance – and tact. 'Constable told me,' Leslie writes, 'that Mr Vernon asked him if the picture on his easel was painted for any particular person; to which he replied: "Yes, sir, it is painted for a *very particular* person – the person for whom I have painted all my life".'

Ironically enough, Constable received his first 'official' recognition in France. 'A prophet is not without honour save in his own country.' Perhaps it was not quite as bad as this; but the fact remains that while the country of his birth refrained from honouring him even by electing him to the Academy, Paris showed his pictures, giving them a place of honour in the exhibition and awarding him the gold medal of merit.

The first news that his work might be shown in Paris was contained in a letter to Fisher in which he told how a Frenchman had called on him and wished to purchase *The Haywain* and *The Bridge*, his object being to make an exhibition of them in Paris where his work was already attracting attention. 'We have agreed as to price, two hundred and

fifty pounds the pair,' wrote Constable, adding, so characteristically, 'and I gave him a small picture of Yarmouth into
the bargain.' Fisher, of course, was delighted for his friend's
sake. 'The purchase of your two great landscapes for Paris,'
he replied, 'is surely a stride up three or four steps of the
ladder of popularity. English boobies, who dare not trust
their own eyes, will discover your merits when they find you
admired in Paris.'

The Paris exhibition was in the spring of 1824; yet,
despite Fisher's optimism, it was not until five years later, in
February, 1829, that Constable was elected an Academician
in this country.

Even then, the belated honour was not without its sting.
The President of the Royal Academy at that time was Sir
Thomas Lawrence, the famous portrait painter, a kind-
hearted enough man, but no great admirer of Constable's
work, a fact which he made painfully obvious when, as in
custom bound on such occasions, Constable called upon
him to pay his respects. Sir Thomas attached great importance to subject-matter in pictures and probably considered
Constable's choice of workaday themes as far too humble.
He therefore made his opinion quite clear that no doubt
Constable would be as surprised at the award as he himself
had been.

All this was very painful to Constable. At fifty-three years
of age, with so great a quantity of work behind him, which
he knew in his heart was far and away the best that England
was now producing, he not unnaturally looked upon the
honour as an act of justice and certainly not of favour.

It had come a year too late, anyway, for the joy of it to be
shared by his wife, who had never lost faith in his genius.
She had died in 1828. And how he must have wished, too,

that the honour could have been bestowed in time to please
his mother, who, when he was still in his early thirties and
quite unknown, had written to him: 'In truth, my dear
John, though in all human probability my head will be laid
low long ere it come to pass, yet with my present light I can
perceive no reason why you should not, one day, with diligence and attention be the performer of a picture worth
£3,000.'

For Constable himself there were not many years now
remaining. His domestic burden was considerable. There
were seven children to provide for, of whom John, the
eldest, was probably his favourite, as he was certainly the
greatest help.

But if Constable's last years were unduly loaded with
worries, they were also years of immense achievement:
nothing seems to have been able to keep him from his
canvases. Of the larger pictures belonging to these years, the
following selection would alone be sufficient to emphasise
the extent of his power and will to let nothing stand in the
way of that fulfilment towards which he had always striven.
Hadleigh Castle was one of the great pictures of this period
– an evocation of the scene of those gaunt Essex ruins, so
turbulent and wild it immediately calls to mind Shake-
speare's *King Lear*. There were also *Stonehenge*, with its
double rainbow arching over the tumbled, druidical temple,
The Cenotaph, in which he caught the recollected emotion
he had experienced on seeing the memorial to the painter
Reynolds which Sir George Beaumont had erected in his
park, and, of course, the famous *Dedham Vale*, where the
scenes that had 'made me a painter' were recreated in one
final glorious moment of vision – the distant view of the
village with its crowning church tower, the trees that love

and knowledge had equally inspired, and the great clouds swirling over. Of each one of these – as of all that had preceded them – how true remain the words of that friend whom Constable once quoted (with such obvious relish) as saying 'he breathes the open air in my pictures, they are more than fresh, they are exhilarating.'

In addition to his continual work in the studio and his care for his children, Constable had now his official duties as an Academician. He was appointed to the hanging committee (a duty which, remembering his own long struggle for recognition, he took with more than ordinary seriousness), and he undertook to write a book, which was completed in 1832, on *English Landscape*.

He does not seem to have allowed himself even the relaxation of reading, certainly not of novels, which never interested him. Two books only are mentioned in Leslie's biography and both are typical of the man: one was Gilbert White's *Selborne*, in which that Hampshire natural historian set down, in elegant language, his original observations of the bird and animal life of his parish, and the poet Cowper's *Letters*, of which Constable said, 'He is an author I prefer to almost any other and when with him I always feel the better for it.'

It was only natural that Constable, whose desk would be littered with feathers and stones and twigs and different coloured samples of earth picked up on his walks, should delight in so exact and observant a naturalist as White of Selborne, whilst the piety and moral sense of the poet Cowper could not fail to appeal to one whose whole life was disciplined to the strict observance of his duty.

A proper humility, too, was inherent in his fine nature. 'Remember,' he once wrote to Leslie, 'the Great were not made for me, nor I for the Great; things are better as they are. My limited and abstracted art is to be found under every hedge and in every lane, and therefore nobody thinks it worth picking up.' His solace was that he knew he was following the way that was best for him. 'The language of the heart is the only one that is universal,' he said; and, in the knowledge that his own pictures spoke 'from the heart to the heart,' he had his satisfaction.

Nature had long ago given him his first schooling in this language of the heart – as long ago as those days when, in solitude or in the sympathetic company of John Dunthorne the glazier, he had dawdled in the meadows within sight of his father's mill, noting with love 'the sound of water escaping from mill-dams, willows, old rotten planks and slimy posts.' In a letter to Maria he had written then, 'I live almost wholly in the fields, and see nobody but the harvest men.' He was saturating his senses with that natural beauty which he was presently to simulate in his canvases – 'light, dews, breezes, bloom, and freshness.' It was his ambition, he said, to get into his pictures that 'sparkle with repose' which, as a boy and lad, he had first learned to appreciate in the wide, green scene of the countryside around Dedham. His ambition calls to mind the words of another nature-lover, this time a writer, Richard Jefferies, who was to do in words what Constable had done in colours. 'I would endeavour,' Jefferies said, before he had even embarked upon his first book, 'to bring in some of the glamour – the magic of sunshine, and green things, and calm waters – if I could.' He too succeeded in his ambition, no less.

And the success of both of them, Jefferies and Constable, writer and painter, was based on the same joyous, yet strictly disciplined, observation of nature in all her moods. They

were both out-of-door men, and their aims were the same;
with Jefferies it was to bring the sunshine into his pages, so
that it should put out the printed word and leave only the
sense of the open air, and with Constable it was to blow the
clouds across his canvas, so that the miller might, as it were,
set his sails by them, and to send the rain scudding across his
painted skies so that Varley, standing before the picture on
the wall, should call for his umbrella.

William Morris

I T IS considered a belittling thing to say of a man that he is a jack of all trades and a master of none. The implication is that if he wishes to make a name for himself in the world he had better stick to one job and shut his eyes to everything that might entice him away from it. Concentration, ruthless and continual, is absolutely essential to the achievement of greatness.

Yet there have been exceptions, though very few. There have been men who, if not exactly jacks of all trades and masters of none, did not give their utmost to any one of the several tasks they undertook but who nevertheless achieved greatness.

Such a man was William Morris. In the course of a fairly long and always vigorous life he tackled so many kinds of jobs that (if the popular saying were infallible) he ought never to have made a name for himself in any one of them. The facts, however, are quite the opposite. Although William Morris died more than half a century ago, his name is still among the best-known in the land. Admittedly, his work, whether of his hands or of his imagination, is already largely out of fashion; but his name and fame still live on and his influence is still felt at a thousand points.

In his lifetime Morris was so many things. He was a story-teller; a poet; a weaver; a designer; a manufacturer of stained glass and painted tiles, of chintzes and tapestries; a printer and a publisher; a politician, a lecturer; and even a street-corner orator.

It would scarcely be thought possible that one man could do and be so many things in a lifetime. And if he was not quite a genius at any one of them, at none of them was he less than good. His poems were sufficiently fine to delight a wide public and eventually to procure for him the offer (which he refused) of the Poet Laureateship. His designs were new and, like his stuffs, of such beauty that no man of taste and sufficient wealth considered his house properly furnished if it did not contain examples of them. His books, for the excellence of their type and the beauty of their binding, for their rich illuminations and decorations, became immediately collectors' pieces of great price. His stories ran into several editions, and at least one of them, *News from Nowhere*, has had a considerable influence over many years. Even his political speeches were memorable both for the revolutionary ideas they expressed and for the fire and conviction with which they were delivered.

And yet into none of these things did Morris put himself wholly, without stint, without reservation; not one of them was so important to him, so passionately absorbing, that nothing of him was left over for anything else.

For this his work is now paying the price. His poetry, except for a few short lyrics, is hardly readable today. His beautifully coloured chintzes and wall-papers, though still admired, are out of fashion in the home. His socialism, which was the driving-force behind everything he did and said, is no longer revolutionary, and we have long since discovered all the flaws in it. Indeed, so far as his actual work is concerned, it might almost be considered a splendid failure.

In spite of this, however, Morris's influence has been as profound as that of any man of his century. For the truth is that he was greater than his work.

His work, however far it fell short of final genius, was necessary because it was the means by which he illustrated in practice the theories he preached and so whole-heartedly believed in; and perhaps it should be judged less for its actual merits than for the enormous and beneficial influence which it exerted.

Morris's position has been admirably summed up by G H D Cole in the following words:

'He had great force; but he dissipated it over so many things that it was never fully concentrated anywhere. Could he have concentrated it more, he might have been a greater artist; and yet the concentration would have been a misfortune. For it was William Morris's mission to throw himself into a great many arts, exhausting none, but creating everywhere things at the least passably beautiful and at the best also powerfully influential for good. I like best to think of him as the man who, loving beauty, wanted to make beauty a common possession of all mankind, and, realising how much stood in the way, did not shrink from giving battle to giants.'

There you have Morris the man, his lack and his worth.

Don Quixote, the hero of Cervantes' famous novel of chivalry, tilted against windmills, his crazed brain mistaking them for warriors. There was nothing crazed about William Morris when, with all the might he possessed, he tilted, not against windmills, but against machines. He saw the machine as the great new enemy of mankind.

In the 'eighties, when he was at the peak of his powers, the machine was admittedly still in its infancy; even so, a farsighted and visionary man could see how it was rapidly growing up and taking over. Soon, unless something were done to stay its progress, it would assume power altogether and man would be reduced to the position of slave. That, anyway, was Morris's fear. He saw all around him the craftsman being superseded by the machine, the workshop by the factory. He saw man losing the cunning of his hands, whereby, until now, he had made lovely and enduring and useful things. And the result everywhere was the triumph of ugliness – ugly buildings, ugly furniture, ugly stuffs, ugly books – where once the hand had made them things of beauty.

And, worst of all, he saw man rapidly losing that happiness in his work which can only come when he is allowed to create. The machine was killing the creator in every man, and as a result work was becoming more and more monotonous and soul-destroying as the machine took over from the hand.

There is a passage in the Bible, in the Book of Ecclesiasticus, with which Morris must have been familiar. It describes the various craftsmen – the carpenter, the smith, the potter – and it praises their skill and diligence, who seek always perfection. 'All these men trust in their hands: and every one is wise in his work. Without these cannot a city be inhabited; and they shall not dwell where they will, nor go up and down. They shall not be sought for in public counsel, nor sit high in the congregation: they shall not sit on the judge's seat, nor understand the sentence of judgment: they cannot declare justice and judgment; and they shall not be found where parables are spoken. *But they will maintain the state of the world, and all their desire is in the work of their craft.*'

Morris saw how this was already no longer true in England and elsewhere: the simple craftsman, trusting in his hands, no longer maintained 'the state of the world' – the machine was doing it for him; and doing it, Morris believed, badly, even disastrously. And all his endeavour, whether he was weaving cloth, or printing books, writing his poems and romances or speaking in the parks and at the street corner, was directed towards the single aim of halting the progress of the machine while yet there was time. His strength lay in the fact that he not only preached, but also practised what he preached: the word and the deed were one in him.

Yet, as we can now see, he was defending a cause that was already lost. Half a century has passed since his death and that comparatively short time has nevertheless been long enough to witness the machine attain a status such as Morris never even dreamed possible. He was a Canute seeking to hold back the flood; and although he even guessed that this might be so, he never guessed how mighty the flood would be.

The machine has taken over. The hand has little more to do, already, than to press the button. To Morris ours would seem like a nightmare world. He believed, with all his heart and mind, that the creative impulse was natural to every man, and that the machine, by denying him the use of his hands, was suppressing this necessary and even vital attribute.

He believed, too, that man was only really happy in his work when he was *making* something – something which should grow under his fingers as the spirit dictated; and that the machine, by doing everything for him, was destroying his chances of achieving true happiness.

Perhaps there was a fundamental fault in Morris's reasoning. Is it true, for instance, that the creative impulse is to be found in everybody and only needs releasing in skilled and rewarding work, as the flower unfolds in the sunshine, and slowly ripens into fruit? And is it necessarily true that machinery is man's curse? Does it not rather depend upon how the machine is used – or abused? Certainly the point is a debatable one, though Morris would never have admitted that it is.

Morris allowed no sort of compromise. He saw a beacon ahead and followed it undeviatingly. He thought he knew what the right and the wrong of the matter was, and nothing had power to shift him from his point of view. This was not so much obstinacy as vision; and of course, if he had not been so single-minded in his vision, so totally unable to see the other side, he would not have been the tremendous influence he was.

The machine today may have triumphed; but its triumph would have been more harmful than it has been if Morris had not given warning of the danger. The standards of general taste may have declined in many ways; but they would have declined still further and in many more ways if Morris had not, by the high standards of his own working examples, given us the means of comparison.

To carry such an ideal through a whole lifetime, as Morris did, requires a stamina far above the ordinary. He met with ridicule and opposition. He lost money right and left. He was even arrested by the police and appeared in Court. But nothing daunted him. The truth is that his strength of character was matched by his strength of body. He was never still – even at meals he would get up and walk about the room. He had a violent temper, which seemed to render him insensitive to pain, so that he would drive his head against a wall and dent the plaster. The tale is told, and doubtless it is true, how one day in his workshop he was angry with a workman and picked up an enormous, vellum-bound and illuminated book (which, by the way, was so precious to him that he allowed nobody to touch it) and hurled it at the offending man's head: it missed and splintered the panels of the wall behind him.

His biographer, J W Mackail, tells how 'once when describing how he had seen passengers staggering off a Channel steamer loaded with luggage, he illustrated his point to the amusement and horror of his audience by getting a chair under each arm and then stooping and lifting the coal-scuttle in his teeth.' His energy, too, was abounding. From deep sleep he would wake and be immediately all alive – in ten minutes he was dressed and had begun the business of the day. It would be worth emphasising this trait of strength and energy if only because so many of his followers and earnest disciples, in after years, have been chiefly noticeable for their pale gentility, to the considerable detriment of the cause which their master lived and died for. There was nothing pale and genteel about Morris, nothing in the least arty-crafty: he was a giant in more than bodily strength.

Morris was born in 1834, of wealthy, middle-class parents, and spent his boyhood in Essex, first at Walthamstow, and then, from the age of six onwards, at Woodford Hall, close against Epping Forest. These were perhaps his most impressionable years: at any rate, he never lost his affection for Essex and especially for the Forest. 'I was born and bred in its neighbourhood,' he wrote, some fifty years later, 'and when I was a boy and young man knew it yard by yard, from Wanstead to the Theydons, and from Hale End to the Fairlop Oak. In those days it had no worse foes than the gravel-stealer and the roving fence-maker, and was always interesting and often very beautiful.' In his books, also, he paid tribute to its groves of horn-beam trees, then as now the outstanding feature of the Forest. Epping Forest was far wilder and lovelier in Morris's young days than it is today, and no doubt his sensitive, poetic spirit was greatly nourished in the deep green privacy of its glades.

Morris was sent to Marlborough College, then but recently founded, and became acquainted there with another forest; but Savernake, under the wide, chalky Downs, could never charm away his affection for Epping; and eagerly, at the end of term, he hurried back to the scenes that had come to mean so much to him. But in 1846 when his father died, and the family moved to Water House, Walthamstow, the Forest became a memory only.

Even as a schoolboy Morris was always writing stories – or, if not writing them, telling them. 'On his walks,' Mackail says, 'he invented and poured forth endless stories, vaguely described as "about Knights and fairies," in which one adventure rose out of another, and the tale flowed on from day to day over a whole term.'

In 1853 he went up to Oxford and there his passion for telling aloud impromptu stories was deflected into another channel: he became well-known for his rich, sonorous readings from the poets. He also became well-known for the ferocity and force with which he played the game of 'single-stick.' 'In defence,' one friend said of him, 'he was unskilful, but vehement and iron-handed in attack. I bore for years after discolourations that were due to his relentless onsets.' But this was, as it were, a mere letting-off of steam. He may not have been conscientious at attending lectures, but his vigorous brain was always at work, exploring, developing, crystallising that attitude to life which presently was to colour and inform all he did and was.

His mother had intended him to take Holy Orders, but by 1855, when he was twenty-two, he knew in his heart that this was not what he was suited to: instead, he decided to become an architect. He had long shown a special interest in old churches; but it was rather in the nature of a specialist's interest; and a year's apprenticeship, under a well-known architect, was sufficient to convince him that neither was this his true vocation.

All his early years, in fact, until in 1859 when he married Jane Burden at the age of twenty-six, were years of self-exploration. After giving up architecture (at least as a profession) he became a painter; but this too turned out to be an infatuation rather than an enduring love. His friend Burne-Jones had introduced him to the great Pre-Raphaelite poet and painter, Dante Gabriel Rossetti, and, under this colourful and forceful influence, he progressed so far in the art of painting as to join with others in providing frescoes for the new Hall of the Oxford Union.

And all the while, Morris was writing poetry. Perhaps if it had come less easily to him, if he could have learned to discipline himself to the rigours of genuine poetic composition - pouring his whole self into it instead of that bit of him which happened just then to be disengaged - he might have made poetry his life's work, his master achievement. But as a poet he was too facile with words: only occasionally did he climb from the levels of charming verse to the heights of poetry. The result inevitably was that his poetry-making did not basically satisfy him, any more than architecture did, or painting. But when he married and set about the task of founding a home, he suddenly discovered himself: he knew now what he wanted to do.

Morris bought an orchard and meadow in the village of Upton, not far from Abbey Wood, and there, to his own design and under the professional supervision of an architect friend, Philip Webb, he built a house. He called it Red House.

He wanted this to be the house of his dreams, the proving point of all his theories with regard to design, furniture, decoration, and so forth: it was to be perfect in every detail. And so the trouble began. Perfection was more or less possible in the building itself, since he and Webb saw eye to eye on the matter and the one could translate the other's ideas into practice; but when it came to furnishing and decorating the house, Morris found himself thwarted at every turn. Neither in kind nor in quality were the available materials, furniture and fittings up to the standard he demanded.

Victorian vulgarity – sheer bad taste – was then at its peak; and in addition, the machine, which was rapidly taking over from the craftsman, imposed shoddy standards everywhere. Colours were bad; design and workmanship were both unworthy.

And so in the end Morris decided that if he could not get what he wanted from the shops and factories, he would make it himself. A company of decorators should be formed, a co-operative band of fellow-artists and craftsmen, whose aim would be the revival of good taste: they would make by hand furniture and fittings and materials of so fine a quality that not only would Morris's own high standards be satisfied but they would gradually impose them on others. Morris and Company was the name given to this idealist adventure, and today its wares have become collectors' pieces. The workshops were situated in Queen Square, a backwater of London's Soho which had been a residential quarter of distinction in the days of Queen Anne but had now fallen out of fashion. The actual building has since been swallowed up in a hospital, but the same type of house – with its porticoed doors and long windows, its panelled rooms and fine staircases – may still be seen in the neighbourhood.

At No 26, therefore, in 1865, under the energetic supervision of Morris himself, the Company began its work of weaving, dyeing, and printing on cloth, and of designing and manufacturing furniture (especially, at first, church furniture) and stained glass. Among Morris's associates in the venture were such well-known artists as Burne-Jones and Madox Brown and Dante Gabriel Rossetti; but Morris was the prime mover, the force round which the whole scheme centred. It was also his money that kept it alive during the first three or four years until the business began to show a profit.

These were anxious years, and yet it is probable that at no time in his life was Morris happier. He had found what he wanted to do. Not only did the craftsman in him discover an outlet, but he had the zealot's joy of knowing that he was doing something vital towards the counteraction of bad style and lack of quality which were yearly growing more rampant throughout the country.

In addition to the fulfilling of customers' orders, work on the furnishing and decorating of Red House went on apace, until it actually assumed the beauty Morris had envisioned for this house of his dreams.

But dreams are not always a sound foundation for a practical venture; and after only five years, Red House had reluctantly to be abandoned. The place proved unhealthy and awkward to get at: soon it became evident that either

Red House or the business in Queen Square must be given up; and of course it was unthinkable that the business, now soundly established, should be dropped.

The blow was in part mitigated by the fact that at heart Morris was an incorrigible Londoner, and he very soon adjusted himself to the idea of living in Queen Square – at least for the time being. Moreover, when the tedious daily journey was done with, he had more time and energy for work; and he was a demon for work. 'Tempestuous and exacting,' one of his friends described him; and not only did he drive himself, like a fury, but he drove others as well. Ruddy-faced and stocky, he was a man of great physical strength. And he was always unconventional. If he had now given up some of the flamboyant indiscretions he had affected in the Oxford days – purple trousers and flowing ties – he was still, in his middle 'thirties, an intense individualist. For awhile he was a director of a mining company (from which much of his income derived) and had to attend Directors' Meetings in a top hat; and the story goes that when he resigned and came home from the last meeting, he solemnly sat on his top hat and never wore one again.

All his life Morris took the keenest delight in old buildings, whether church or castle, mansion or cottage. He loved them as an expression of an England that was passing, an England where master craftsmen gave free expression to the innate good taste, building houses that did indeed look as if 'some heart were in their stone.'

Even as a young man he had spent a lot of time going over old churches, and loudly he railed against the bad taste with which so many of them had recently been restored. Much of the fine work carried out by Morris and Company, in fact, was for churches and colleges: it was Morris's way of taking a practical lead in defending these old buildings from the restorer's ignorant and desecrating hand. Even Red House, of course, had been in part a demonstration against the architectural ugliness which was in the ascendant and with which England's fine old country houses so sharply contrasted.

It was not surprising, therefore, that sooner or later he felt the need to own and care for some such old country house, to which he could escape, for refreshment of mind and spirit, from the nervous strain and restless activities of Queen Square. The Manor House at Kelmscott was his final choice, and for twenty-five years this beautiful old Gloucestershire house was his country home.

Kelmscott Manor stands on the upper reaches of the Thames, not far from Lechlade. Even today it is remote and quiet – a green, forsaken corner of rural England – and in Morris's time it was even lonelier. The nearest railway was at Witney; and every time Morris came down to Kelmscott from London, in search of peace and quiet, he had to finish the journey with a long ride through the Berkshire hills, as if so fine a reward as Kelmscott were not to be won without due endeavour.

It was an Elizabethan house, built of stone, and full of character. The limestone belt that runs across England, from Dorset to Yorkshire, excels, generally, in good architecture, especially in the south-western region. It is almost as if, having so excellent a stone to work with, those early builders could not go wrong. Everything about those old houses is lovely and comely, from the steep gables, with their decorated finials, to the shapely drip-stones over the windows, and from the stone tiles on the roofs to the ample porch welcoming the visitor.

No wonder Morris was ecstatic when he found Kelmscott that spring day in 1871. He wrote at once to a friend: 'I have been looking about for a house for the wife and kids, and whither do you guess my eye is turned now? Kelmscott, a little village about two miles above Radcott Bridge – a heaven on earth; an old stone Elizabethan house like Water Eaton, and such a garden! Close down on the river, a boat house and all things handy.' Morris was often to try and put on paper, in later years, the pleasure Kelmscott always excited in him, and one of the best descriptions comes from *News from Nowhere*, that vision of Arcadia in which he summed up his hopes for a better and happier life for mankind.

But before Morris could enter into the full enjoyment of his new home, he had first to go to Iceland, whose poems and sagas had long attracted him. From this wild journey, so graphically recorded in a long journal, he brought home with him a little Iceland pony called Mouse. One of his children later gave this account of Mouse in his happy exile.

He was gentle and quiet, though not without slyness; for I remember there was one gatepost against which, when I went out for a ride, he used often to try to rub me off his broad back. I'm ashamed for my horsemanship to think how often the rogue had his way. Father used to ride him about the country a good bit at first. Then I jogged about with him, and he used to be put to a little basket-carriage, and go meandering along in a meditative way. He got enormously fat on our coarse thick plentiful English grass, with little to do; and I used to imagine him lonely and yearning for the fun and clatter and hardships of his Iceland life among his friends, as he stood there with his head stretched forward looking intensely meditative. One day, when the hunt passed through our home meadows, the excitement of horses and hounds was too much for the lonely philosopher: he threw up his head, and, fat as he was, bundled over a hedge and actually followed the hounds a good way. I missed the gentle funny little animal much when he died.

If those lush Gloucestershire meadows were too peaceful for Mouse, Kelmscott Manor itself was almost too peaceful for Morris – at least for too long at a time. So he kept a study and bedroom in Queen Square, tucked in among his increasingly busy and prosperous workshops.

The activities he engaged in during these years of his prime – reviving the lost art of dyeing, illuminating scripts on vellum, writing long poems based on the Iceland sagas, lecturing, speaking at political meetings – would have been enough for several men of ordinary fire and energy. Perhaps the most surprising of these activities was the political one. Artists and poets, especially in the nineteenth century, were not usually actively concerned with politics. But Morris was a reformer as well as an artist: the dynamic urge behind all his art was the desire to make men more appreciative of beautiful things. So he joined the Liberal Party and for a time was very active on its behalf; but by 1880 he had already fallen foul of it and turned his attention to Socialism.

As it happened, however, his most useful social activity during these years was not political at all: it was his foundation, in 1877, of the Society for the Protection of Ancient Monuments.

Wholesale destruction of ancient buildings, either out of sheer barbarism or in the guise of restoration, was going on throughout the country, and nobody seemed to be able to do anything about it. The damage was particularly widespread in connection with churches; and it was the announcement that Tewkesbury Abbey, one of England's finest ecclesiastical buildings, was about to be 'restored' that finally roused Morris to action. The demon of the piece was Sir Gilbert Scott, an architect whose so-called restoration of churches throughout the land did more than anything else to ruin our national heritage of noble old buildings.

My eye just now caught the word restoration in the morning paper (Morris wrote to the *Athenaeum*, hot with anger) and, on looking closer, I saw that this time it is nothing less than the Minster of Tewkesbury that is to be destroyed by Sir Gilbert Scott. Is it too late to do something to save it – it and whatever else of beautiful and historical value is still left to us on the sites of the ancient buildings we were once so famous for? Would it not be of some use, once for all, and with the least possible delay, to set on foot an association for the purpose of watching over and protecting these relics, which, scanty as they are now become, are still wonderful treasures, all the more priceless in this age when the newly-invented study of living history is the chief joy of so many of our lives?

Within a month of Morris's appeal, the Society for the Protection of Ancient Buildings had been constituted, Morris himself acting as secretary. Perhaps the name of the Society was a little pompous: at any rate, Morris always referred to it thereafter as 'our Anti-scrape Society.' Incalculable good has been done, in a quiet way, by this inspired effort to save our fine old buildings from destruction, and the good work still goes on. Incidentally, the present head-offices of the Society for the Protection of Ancient Monuments, as it is now called, are in Great Ormond Street, London, not a stone's throw from the site of Morris's workshops of three-quarters of a century ago.

One of the most likeable things about Morris was his readiness, whenever possible, to join in a spree. He was all eagerness, therefore, when his family one day in the summer of 1880 proposed a trip by boat from Hammersmith to Kelmscott. That, he felt, would be a homecoming indeed. Accordingly, the *Ark*, as the boat was called, was duly fitted out and made ready for the journey.

'Imagine,' (wrote Morris) 'a biggish company boat with a small omnibus on board, fitted up luxuriously inside with two shelves and a glass rack, and a sort of boot behind this: room for two rowers in front, and I must say for not many more except in the cabin or omnibus. Still, what joy (to a little mind) to see the landscape out of a square pane of glass and to sleep a-nights with the stream rushing two inches past one's ear. Then after all, there is the romance of the bank, and outside the boat the world is wide.'

So the party drifted on, past Hampton Court, Eton, Maidenhead, Cookham, Henley, Wallingford and Oxford. One of them would steer, another would pull at the sculls; sometimes Morris (who fancied himself as a cook) prepared the meals, sometimes he gave himself up to the enjoyment of the scene as it drifted past – the little village churches in their trees, the work at the various locks, the holiday-makers, and the harvesters filling their punts with sedges. And at last they came to Radcott itself: they were home. 'Charles was waiting us with a lantern at our bridge by the corner at 10pm, and presently the ancient house had me in its arms again: J had lighted up all brilliantly, and sweet it looked you may be sure.'

The Queen Square workshops were rapidly becoming far too cramped for the amount of orders that now poured into the firm of Morris and Company; and so it was decided to move out of London, though not too far away. At last some disused printing premises were found at Merton, in Surrey, not more than seven miles from Charing Cross. The river Wandle ran through the grounds, and this itself was a recommendation, since water was essential for dyeing.

The move was made in the summer of 1881, and Morris turned out a whole series of designs for chintzes (many of them among his best) ready for the new works to start on. A prospectus issued from the firm about this time gives an idea of the varied activities engaged upon by Morris and Company. The list includes painted glass windows, hand-woven tapestries, carpets, embroideries, tiles, furniture, printed cotton goods, paper hangings, velvets and cloths, upholstery and general house decorations.

Even all this, however, was not sufficient to satisfy Morris: more and more he gave his time and energy to the cause of Socialism, editing the journal of the Socialist League, writing articles, lecturing up and down the country, and speaking at street corners.

'I have been living,' he wrote in 1883, 'in a sort of storm of newspaper brickbats.' But sometimes the brickbats were rather less theoretical. At some of his street corner meetings he came into conflict with the police, and was even marched off to the police station, charged with disorderly conduct and striking a policeman – a charge that was later withdrawn. Morris accepted it all good-humouredly enough, as part and parcel of the cause which was his life's ambition, namely, to help as much as he could, and by whatever way he could, to free men from the bondage of the machine, which, as he saw it, was not only robbing them of the beauty that was their heritage but was actually turning them into slaves. He wanted men to cast out the machine, however productive and labour-saving it might be, and demand again, as their right, work that they would enjoy doing.

It was, of course, a battle against hopeless odds. The machine, however furiously Morris might deplore it, had come to stay: time could not run backwards. But the reformer, the zealot, admits no compromise. Things are either black or white, right or wrong. Morris could not see, and would not have admitted it if he could, that the curse of the machine lies not so much in itself as in the way it is abused for the exploitation, one way or another, of mankind. Nor is it possible for all men to be craftsmen, engaged in work they enjoy doing: the impulse to create, which Morris affirmed was common to everybody, is, in fact, limited to a comparatively few people.

These, no doubt, are flaws in Morris's argument, weaknesses in the cause for which he spent himself, body and soul; but the strength of his appeal, the good he did, far outweighs any such flaws and weaknesses. He called a halt to the vulgarity of the time. He opened men's eyes, by the example of his own work, to beauty – especially beauty of good design and true colour. He reminded them of the danger they were running in abandoning the craftsman in favour of the machine; and by so doing at least he gave heart to small groups of people, all over the country, who kept alive the flame of his ideal.

The one book of his that did more than any other (and more than his poems, his lectures and pamphlets) to popularise his ideal was perhaps the Utopian romance called *News from Nowhere.* It was published towards the end of his life, in 1891, though it had already appeared, in serial form, in *The Commonweal.*

'It cannot be too often repeated,' Morris wrote, 'that the true incentive to useful and happy labour is, and must be, pleasure in the work itself.' And it was to show the possibilities of a world in which this rule prevailed that he wrote *News from Nowhere.* Slight as it is, its happy pastoral pictures remain vividly in the reader's mind: it is impossible to close the book without feeling that human life could and should be happier than it is, if only man would pay less attention to his material means and more to his spiritual. Like all Utopian romances it is a dream; but it is a dream behind which there is a lot of common sense; a dream, moreover, which men would do well to heed the meaning of.

'Go back,' the book ends, 'and be the happier for having seen us, for having added a little hope to your struggle. Go on living while you may, striving, with whatsoever pain and labour needs must be, to build up little by little the new day of fellowship, and rest, and happiness.'

After the publication of this book, Morris had but five more years to live. Poet, story-teller, artist, craftsman, politician, he was all of these; but he himself gave as his profession that of designer. At any rate, there is a fitness in the fact that his last years were spent in the peaceful (if anything to do with Morris could be said to be peaceful) occupation of preparing for the Kelmscott Press a new edition of Chaucer, the poet whom he had always particularly enjoyed.

For six years this project was rarely out of Morris's mind, and the actual production of it took three and a half years. The Kelmscott Chaucer was to be as beautiful a book as could possibly be devised, worthy of the poet, and worthy, too, to rank along with those mediaeval Books of the Hours, Psalters, and other monkish volumes whose vellum pages, so exquisitely decorated and so beautifully scripted, had given Morris such continual delight.

His lifelong friend, Burne-Jones, was to do the pictures, eighty-seven of them. Morris himself would do the initial letters, borders and ornamentation. And everything, from the type the book was printed in to the white pigskin binding and silver clasps, was to be the work of the best of the craftsmen whom Morris's genius had gathered about him.

There were, of course, the usual delays, and Morris chafed under them as he had always done. Perhaps the delays irked him more than ever now, since he seemed somehow to sense that his time was running out. But at last, in June of 1896, the first two copies were ready, one for Burne-Jones, one for Morris himself. It was his last finished work – the supreme memorial to his genius. On October 3rd of the same year, in his beloved old Cotswold manor house, with his devoted friends about him, he died. The busy brain was still now, the clever hands idle. 'He led us all a dance,' as one of his fellow-workmen said; 'would he could lead us some more!'

Captain Oates

GESTINGTHORPE IS a little village on the north border of Essex. From far afield you can see the Tudor brick tower of its church, sixty-six feet tall. And if you climb inside as far as the bells, you can see that the fifth and sixth of the peal are inscribed 'in gratitude to God for the safe return with honour of my beloved son from the dangers of the war in South Africa.' The soldier was Captain Lawrence Edward Grace Oates, of the Inniskilling Dragoons.

Then, if you turn round and peer through the slats of one of the windows in the tower, you can see the house itself to which he safely returned. Gestingthorpe Hall – or Over Hall, as it is properly called – had been his home since he was eleven years old. It is a fine old house, almost buried in trees, with a small park outside the high walls of the garden.

But Captain Oates was to face much greater dangers than the war in South Africa. And from these he did not return. In the nave of the church, when you have climbed down the ladders from the tower, you can see on the south wall a brass tablet that tells, in a few words, the story of those later dangers. This is what it says:

'In memory of a very gallant gentleman, Lawrence Edward Grace Oates, Captain in the Inniskilling Dragoons, born March 17th, 1880, died March 17th, 1912, on the return journey from the South Pole of the Scott Antarctic Expedition. When all were beset by hardship, he being gravely injured went out into the blizzard to die, in the hope that by so doing he might enable his comrades to reach safety.'

The bells, after having been silent for three-quarters of a century, because they were unsafe, were restored (in 1901) by Captain Oates' mother; and the tablet in the nave was placed there (in 1913) by his brother officers of the Inniskilling Dragoons.

He was both soldier and explorer – and, as either, he was equally brave. As a soldier he was known as 'No Surrender Oates'; and as an explorer the praise of his courage and self-sacrifice rang round the world. He was the Sir Philip Sidney of our time.

There are many memorials to him: a portrait medallion at Eton, for instance, where he went to school; Oates College for boys, in the Argentine; and Oates Land, near the South Pole. But of all the memorials perhaps he would have been proudest of the bells that peal out over his little home village and of the brass tablet in the nave of its church.

For the story of Captain Oates really begins and ends in Gestingthorpe. There, as a boy, he learned the mastery of horses that was to prove so invaluable when he joined Scott's Antarctic Expedition and was put in charge of the ponies upon which so much depended; and it was of Gestingthorpe, and of his mother who awaited him there, that he spoke on that last evening when he sat in the tent with his comrades, imprisoned by the shrieking blizzard, waiting to die.

Did he remember then the stables at the back of the Hall, where he had spent some of the happiest hours of his life? They are still there, with the same bell-turret and the same weather-cock turning in the wind. And did he think of the garden, and the pond with its tiny island, and the statue of the little boy pulling a thorn out of his foot? These too are still there among the heavy trees where the rooks come cawing home at dusk.

Next to horses, Lawrence Oates loved ships and the sea. Even before he was eleven years old, he had three times made the voyage to South Africa, for his health. His father owned a 40-ton yacht, the *Curlew*, and Lawrence had been accustomed to sailing from his earliest days. It was his ambition to have a ship of his own; and when he was eighteen, he and his brother between them bought an 18-ton yawl, the *Saunterer*.

The rougher the weather, the better Lawrence seemed to like it – despite the fact that he was always seasick. This sometimes led to trouble. There was that occasion, for example, when the brothers and a crew of two were bound for Antwerp. They lay wind-bound at Dover for four days, and still the gale showed no signs of dying down. Lawrence was impatient to put to sea. 'If you go,' said Bryan, 'you go alone.' And so he went without his brother. But the journey was so rough that the crew left him at Antwerp, grumbling that they had had enough and would return by steamer.

When the storm subsided, however, they had second thoughts and offered to sail the *Saunterer* back to England. 'No,' said Lawrence: 'you said you were going; now go!' But they persisted, and in the end he let them sail with him. 'But when we land,' he said, 'I am finished with you.'

Already his strength of character was showing itself. There was nothing about him now of the delicate youth who had had to take sea-voyages for his health and who, after two years at Eton, fell sick of pneumonia and never went back to school. The open air life had done its work; he was ready to face anything. Never much good at his lessons, he had learned other things than those the books can teach.

Despite his fondness for ships and the sea, he had always wanted to be a soldier, especially, of course, a soldier in a cavalry regiment, where he could continue to use his skill in horsemanship.

Yet it was not until 1900, after he had served for two years in the West Yorkshire Militia, that his wish came true. The war in South Africa had been going badly: the British suffered one defeat after another at the hands of the Boers. Oates longed to go and take his share. He put in for a commission, and waited and waited. Then the tide of war began to turn in our favour. The siege of Ladysmith was raised; the fierce old Boer leader, Cronje, surrendered; Bloemfontein was invested; Mafeking was saved. It began to look as if the fighting would all be over before Oates got a chance.

But on May 30th, 1900, he was posted to the 6th Inniskilling Dragoons. Soon he would get his sailing orders, he thought. But in fact it was not until seven months later that, together with two other subalterns, fifty troopers, and the regimental band, he finally landed in Cape Town. Almost immediately the draft was sent into action and gave such a good account of itself that Oates was promoted a full Lieutenant and sent to join Colonel Pearson's column for the relief of Aberdeen.

Seeing Colonel Pearson's column approach, the Boers withdrew to the surrounding hills. From there they sniped the cavalry with such deadly effect that it was decided, early in the morning, to send out three patrols, of fifteen men apiece, to check their activities. The Inniskilling patrol was in the charge of Lieut Oates.

What happened is best told in the official account:

> Taking advantage of all cover, Lieut Oates directed
> each man as he finished his ammunition to creep back
> to the town with his rifle; several were seriously
> wounded but managed to crawl away. In the end, after
> four hours' fighting, only Oates himself remained;
> with one of the last shots fired by the enemy, he was
> shot through the thigh, the bone being broken.

> Twice during the engagement Scheepers, who was
> in command of the Boers, had sent a white flag,
> demanding surrender, but on both occasions got the
> same reply, viz, 'That they were there to fight, and not
> to surrender.' At one time the Boers got up to within
> 20 yards of the small party, but finally gave up the
> attempt to capture it, and did not secure a single rifle.

> It was not until 6.30 p.m. that Lieut Oates was
> picked up by the ambulance ... he had lain wounded
> since 10 a.m.

Hence, of course, the nick-name, 'No Surrender Oates.'
Hence, also, the restored peal of bells in Gestingthorpe
church, welcoming him home. But there was more fighting
to be done yet, once he was strong enough to go out again
and rejoin his regiment; and it was not until October 31st,
1902, that he finally left South Africa, with the Queen's
Medal and Five Clasps pinned to his tunic.

India came next; but barrack life, after all the excitement
of campaigning, was dull. If only there were hounds to ride
to! And so, characteristically, he decided to import a pack of
his own.

Across the fields from Gestingthorpe church there is an

old barn; and it was here that Oates and his brother assembled such hounds as they could get hold of, until eventually there were more than the two of them could manage, and they had to employ a kennel-man. In time there were twenty-five couple; these were shipped to Mhow, in India, where the Inniskillings were stationed.

The hounds were used to hunt hyenas. No doubt the natives smiled – those mad Englishmen again! – especially when they saw Oates hunting in a bowler hat. But it was good sport; and the bowler hat was not quite so silly as it looked, for the heavy land cracked in the heat after rain, and a horse could easily pitch its rider.

It was in India, at Delhi, that Oates heard how Captain Scott was preparing a new expedition to the South Pole. Bored, despite his hounds, Oates grasped at the chance. He wrote at once, offering his services, and to his delight Scott replied, asking for qualifications. Oates said he owned a pack of hounds; had studied the use of Manchurian ponies in Tibet; knew a great deal about dogs and horses; and hoped he would prove a fit person to join the expedition.

Scott then invited him to come home and talk the matter over, and leave was duly arranged. Nine years before, Scott had led a similar Antarctic expedition, in the *Discovery*; so he knew exactly the type of man he needed, and saw at once that Oates was of this type – a man of strong character and fine physique and having a special ability with animals.

But the purpose of any exploring expedition is not solely to reach a certain destination. The scientific information which is gathered on the way, may, in fact, turn out to be just as important as the attaining of the goal itself. Whether Scott's expedition should succeed in reaching the South Pole or not, much therefore was hoped of it. Details of temperature, air currents and pressure; of the formations and movements of ice; of the geological history of the mountains – all this would be quite as much part of the job as planting a flag at the Pole.

And so, when Oates was finally accepted, and the War Office had sanctioned his 'special extra-regimental employ with the British Antarctic Expedition,' it was necessary for him to take a course in surveying at the school of the Royal Geographical Society. But his particular task, of course, would be to look after the dogs and ponies.

His pleasure at being accepted can be imagined. He even ventured to express the hope to Captain Scott that he would not be left at the base but would be among those selected to go right on to the South Pole. Scott's reply was typical of the man. He intended, he said, to take with him on the last stages the four fittest men; and if Oates turned out to be one of these, he would certainly have his wish.

By June of 1910, the *Terra Nova* had been fitted out and was ready at Cardiff for sailing to New Zealand. Much of the cost of the expedition had been met by public subscription: indeed, the greatest interest was shown in the whole adventure. Schoolboys subscribed to buy the ponies, sledges, tents and reindeer sleeping-bags, Oates' particular sleeping-bag being given by Trafalgar House School, Winchester.

It took five months to sail to New Zealand – five months of valuable preparation for the men, in getting to know one another, in fitting themselves for their special tasks, and in general training. And by the end of November everything was ready for them to set out from Port Chalmers on the last ocean lap of the journey. The ship was so loaded with gear and provisions that the deck was hardly visible; and below there were thirty-three Siberian dogs, howling and straining at their chains, and nineteen Manchurian ponies. It would be rough going for the animals and Oates – Titus, as he was now generally known – made everything as comfortable for them as he possibly could.

Then the first bad news arrived. Amundsen, the Norwegian explorer who, it had been supposed, was planning an Arctic expedition, telegraphed to Scott to say that he was going to the Antarctic instead. Well, it could not be helped: Scott might get there first, anyway.

The journey from New Zealand to South Victoria Land, where the expedition was to make its base, was already no picnic. Dirty weather seemed to pursue them all the way. Seas washed over the decks, flinging everything about. A dog was drowned, a pony died. Oates had his hands full. One of his shipmates said:

> Those who saw him in the gale will never forget his strong brown face, illuminated by a hanging lamp, as he stood among the suffering beasts. He was a fine, powerful man, and on occasions he seemed to be lifting the poor little ponies to their feet as the ship lurched heavily to leeward and a great sea would wash the legs of his charges from under them. He himself appeared quite unconscious of any personal suffering although his hands and feet must have been absolutely numbed by cold and wet.

By the first week in December, the *Terra Nova* was among the icebergs, some not much more than floes, some as big as islands, ten miles long, and a couple of hundred feet high. Birds of the polar seas began to appear: penguins shuffled across the ice to get a closer view of the intruders.

As the ice increased, the ship would sometimes be held fast for days, and then the men would 'go ashore' for exercise.

Christmas Day found them still ice-bound. They hung the ship with flags, there was a Christmas dinner (including champagne), and afterwards everybody, whether he could sing or not, contributed a song. Oates' contribution, as perhaps befitted an Essex countryman, was 'The Fly is on the Turnip.'

It was New Year's Day before they sighted land. Early in the morning, they came hurrying up on deck, wrapped in blankets, for their first sight of Antarctica. A hundred miles away in the clear air, the rosy peaks of South Victoria Land thrust up into the sky: Mt Sabine, Mt Terror, and Mt Erebus, on a spur of which they would camp.

The excitement of the dogs, when at last they were landed, knew no bounds. They tunnelled in the snow and scratched in the ice and never once stopped barking. Then the ponies were slung out on a yardarm, one at a time; and soon they too were rolling in the snow, for joy at having their freedom again.

The plan was to prepare winter quarters somewhere not far from Hut Point (where Scott had camped in the 1902 expedition) and from there to establish a series of supply depots along the route which they would take as soon as the all-night winter was over. This proved to be a three months' job, involving all sorts of mishaps and delays.

Once an entire dog-team fell into a crevasse, and hung there howling, supported on one side by the leading dog and on the other by the loaded sledge. Eleven of the thirteen dogs were hauled to safety, the other two remaining lodged on a difficult snow-ledge down the crevasse. It was Captain Scott (never one to ask others to do what he would not attempt himself) who climbed down and rescued them. As for the ponies, they fared even worse. Weary Willy, far from sprightly at the best of times, was the first to fall by the way; and by the time the party had got back to winter quarters, only ten of the original seventeen remained alive.

Nor were these the only blows. The *Terra Nova*, unable to wait, for fear of the closing ice, had sailed for New Zealand, leaving Scott a message which could scarcely have been more depressing. During the party's absence, the ship had sailed along the Great Ice Barrier, and there it had been discovered that Amundsen was already established in the Bay of Whales, sixty miles nearer the South Pole than Scott. Moreover, the message added that he was relying on dogs, more fleet and mobile than ponies, and would therefore be able to start sooner.

The Antarctic winter closed in on Scott and his men: for four months now they would have to wait, shut in darkness and bitter cold. But they had made everything as comfortable as they could, both for themselves and for the animals.

They played endless games of backgammon and chess. Sometimes they had music, for there was a gramophone. (There was also a piano; but nobody seemed very expert at playing it.) They even took it in turns to give lectures, each on his special subject – Oates, needless to say, lectured on horses. There were books to read. And always Oates was kept busy looking after his precious charges.

Then on August 23rd the sun appeared, lodged like a spark on the horizon. Of course they had to celebrate. After a special dinner there were speeches; and then a fantastic 'Christmas Tree' was brought in. Wilson, the party's doctor – Uncle Bill, they called him – had made it, out of a ski-stick and penguin feathers, and hung it with candles and gift toys. Appropriately, Captain Oates of the Inniskilling Dragoons got a toy gun, with which, for the rest of the evening, he chased his comrades round the hut, shooting at everybody. In such hard circumstances as these men were enduring, the smallest thing can give pleasure: it all depends upon the spirit in which it is received. 'If you want to please me very much,' said Oates, 'you will fall down when I shoot you.' And so, like little boys at a Christmas Party, these tough and stalwart explorers all fell down.

The first thing to be done, now that light had returned, streaming across the sky in the most beautiful colours, was to get fit again, ready for the great task that lay ahead.

Scott proposed to use the ponies to haul supplies as far as Beardmore Glacier, a distance of over four hundred miles, including the treacherous Great Ice Barrier. Then the ponies would be shot and the men would carry their own supplies on to the Pole and back again to Hut Point.

Oates was no sentimentalist; yet he must have felt sad, knowing the fate that awaited his ponies. Not that they were such a gentle, loveable lot; but he had attended them so long now, through all sorts of difficulties; and anyway it would have been against his nature not to like them. Even Christopher, the worst-tempered of them all. Nobody else could handle Christopher, and even Oates took his life in his hands every time he harnessed him. The poor brutes had already endured so much – let alone what still lay ahead of them.

By the end of September the party was ready to move; and they would need every day of the time till darkness clamped down again; but, what with one thing and another, it was November 1st before they actually got away.

There is hardly any parallel, all over the world, to the

weather on the Great Ice Barrier, and the expedition ran into some of its very worst. Sometimes the sun poured down from a cloudless sky, though the temperature was 20 degrees F below zero. Sometimes they ran into such a blinding, searing blizzard that there was nothing to do but to get into their sleeping-bags and let the days somehow pass until it was over. Sometimes showers of crystals fell on them, making the going even harder than usual and cutting the men's already blistered skin. Washing and shaving, of course, were out of the question; and even to clean their hands in snow involved the risk of frost-bite.

By the fifteenth day they had only done 130 miles. Here they established the first depot. The ponies were feeling it badly; and although, with the establishment of each new depot across the Barrier, their loads became lighter, Oates was about the only man now who believed they might get through to the Glacier. It was as if he would not let them down.

But the endless blizzards began to tell on them so cruelly that one after another of them had to be killed. They held up the party and wasted valuable time. Even Christopher, the toughest of them, had to be shot. At the very entrance to the Glacier, it was obvious that the remaining ponies, too, must go; and so Oates was told to shoot the lot. This was the worst task that so far had come his way. 'I congratulate you, Titus,' said tender-hearted Wilson, when at last it was over. 'And I thank you, Titus,' said Scott, knowing well what Oates' feelings must have been.

Shambles Camp was the name they gave to the place. It is easy to be wise after the event and say that the ponies, as a means of transport in the Antarctic, were a mistake; and in any case it must be remembered that there were still forty years to go before exploration had become so exact a science that even Mt Everest could he assailed with success. Scott's men in the Antarctic, in 1911, had, in comparison with Hunt's men on Mt Everest, in 1953, less than a minimum of scientific and mechanical aid. The value of vitamins and calories, for instance, was hardly appreciated then; and even the motors, from which Scott had expected so much, gave out before the expedition had got away from Hut Point.

Three supply depots were to be established on the Glacier. When the first was established, the dogs were sent home, and the twelve men carried on alone, the three sledges bearing 800 lb apiece. There were still five hundred miles to go, and the brief summer was hurrying by. Across the biggest glacier in the world they battled, down to their singlets now and with crampons on their feet. A lonelier place than this white desert cannot he imagined; and yet in the midst of it two skua gulls suddenly appeared, circling overhead. Had they sensed pony-meat all that way off?

At last the men reached the head of the Glacier, where the first supporting party was to be shed. It was a tense moment for everybody. Who would be the disappointed ones? Scott told them the names of his selected team, and to his immense relief Oates heard his own among them.

So the last stage of the journey began. Christmas morning found them still on the march, for there was no time to waste on celebrations. Hardly had they started when one of them – Lashley was his name – fell into a crevasse. The region was full of crevasses, and the worst of it was that they were often concealed under false bridges of snow. It was Lashley's birthday, as well as Christmas morning, and there he was dangling at the end of his rope, almost dragging the entire crew with him. When at last his comrades had hauled him out of the gaping icy jaws, they wished him many happy returns of the day! If somebody had not noticed, only the day before, that his rope was fraying, so that he took a new one, that birthday would have been his last.

For once in a while the weather, too, was lucky: the party averaged as much as fifteen miles a day. By December 30th they had even made up the lost time. But, had they known it, on that day Amundsen passed them sixty-five miles to the east, on his way home, the spur of victory speeding him on.

Three days later, Scott's party was reduced to five, illness having made it necessary for three to return. There were 146 miles to go and they had food for a month. In his diary Scott left a record of these men who were still with him:

Wilson is always on the look-out to alleviate the small pains and troubles incident to our work ... Evans is a giant worker, with a remarkable headpiece. It is only now I realise how much has been due to him ... Bowers remains a marvel. I leave all the provision arrangements with him. In addition to the stores, he keeps the most thorough and conscientious meteorological record and to this now adds the duties of observer and photographer. Nothing comes amiss to him, and no work is too hard ... Oates had his invaluable period with the ponies. Now he is a foot slogger and goes hard the whole time, does his share of camp work, and stands the hardship as well as any of us. I would not like to be without him either.

The way became harder again, the blizzards returned. All the same, soon there were only 70 miles to go: seven days more and they should reach their objective. In a kind of trance, a deadness, they carried on. Presently there were only 27 miles to go: two good marches now would do it. Victory was almost in sight.

Then 'the worst has happened,' Scott wrote in his diary. For on the morning of January 16th they came upon sledge-tracks and dog-tracks in the snow, some going south, some returning north. It was obvious what had happened. Amundsen had beaten them.

Disappointment is no word for what they must have felt. To have endured so much – and all for this! But, cruelly as the prize had been snatched out of their hands, they must finish what they had set out to do. On they went; and at journey's end they found a tent, with a pile of discarded tackle and the names of the five Norwegians who had got there before them. There was also a letter to King Haakon of Norway, with a request to Scott that, if he should find it, he would deliver it to the King.

The Union Jack was planted in the snow, and photographs were taken. There was a celebration supper – with a bar of chocolate each and a cigarette, Uncle Bill's little surprise, which he had carried with him all that terrible way.

But all the while they were thinking how near they had been to victory. No wonder Scott wrote in his diary: 'Great God, this is an awful place!'

Grimly they turned north and began the long trek home. Nine hundred miles of ice faced them. Their health was undermined, their strength sapped, only incredible determination would see them through. Supplies would await them at each depot, but with nothing to spare for emergencies. And time was against them.

For awhile, however, all went well enough. They used a following wind by making a sail, whose yard, incidentally, was a broken runner from one of Amundsen's sledges. But presently the wind increased so much that braking against it was almost as hard a work as slogging on foot. Evans was clearly breaking up, and Oates was always getting frost-bite now. Then even the wind turned against them. At the best, they had had only two pounds of food per man each day: now it was less. They talked – if they talked at all – of the fine meals they would have when they got back to England.

The sick men caused delays which they simply could not afford. And then Evans gave way altogether. Again and again he collapsed, his mind seemed to fail. They waited for him to recover. Then one day he dragged so far behind that they lost sight of him, and Oates was sent back to find him. He was brought into camp, but nothing could be done for him; and next day he died.

Oates himself was suffering more and more every day; his feet were so badly frost-bitten that nothing could save them; but he struggled on. Worst of all, he realized that he too was now a hindrance on the others. He asked Wilson, to whom they always turned in their troubles, what he should do. 'Slog on, just slog on,' was the only answer he could give; and Oates slogged on, hardly knowing how.

Well enough Scott saw the plight they were in. 'Of course,' he wrote in his diary, 'poor Titus is our greatest handicap.' So he ordered Wilson to give each man thirty opium tablets whereby, if he chose, he might end his misery.

But for ten more days Oates carried on, refusing, like the soldier he was, to take the way out that had been offered. The weather worsened. Even by mid-day the temperature rarely rose above 40 degrees below zero. On one occasion, Oates begged his comrades to leave him behind in his sleeping-bag; but they refused.

So his last night came. He spoke of his mother, at home in Essex. He spoke, too, of his regiment. And then he turned to sleep. The rest must be told in Scott's own words:

> He was a brave soul. He slept through the night, hoping not to wake, but he awoke in the morning. It was blowing a blizzard. Oates said, 'I am just going outside, and I may be some time.' We knew he was walking to his death; but though we tried to dissuade him, we knew it was the act of a brave man and an English gentleman.

The day was March 17th, 1912, his thirty-second birthday.

The three remaining men went on. They covered fifteen miles and could do no more. Then, with only two days' food, they tried again; but again they had to give up. They were eleven miles from One Ton Camp – eleven miles too many. A raging blizzard kept them in their tent, and by the 29th it still showed no signs of slackening.

On that day Scott made his last entry in the diary:

> Had we lived, I should have had a tale to tell of the endurance and courage of my companions which would have stirred the heart of every Englishman. These rough notes and our dead bodies must tell the tale.

... It was many months before a search-party was able to set out over the barren ice-fields in an attempt to find the place of Oates' heroic death. On a rough tablet they carved his name and then added, 'Hereabouts died a very gallant gentleman. R.I.P.' Those simple words, like the deed they told, soon echoed round the world – and are echoing still.